Made for Eternity -

Study Outline

MADE FOR ETERNITY -
STUDY OUTLINE

DR. WALKER WALKER

Optional Dr. Walker Walker
P. o. Box 618761
Orlando, FL 32861
E-mail: kwaler@yahoo.com

Cover design by Jhameek Walker
(Copyright reserved)

SMJ Publishing

ISBN:0692402047
ISBN 13:9780692402047

TABLE OF CONTENTS

1. How to Use this Study Outline

1. Each chapter in this study outline is accompanied by devotional guides including, prayers, selected hymns, scriptures, chapter objectives, general overviews, and numbered points. Each chapter is also broken down into topics, subtopics, and sections that are accompanied by suggested evaluation and discussion questions for interactive and participative learning.

2. The introduction and chapters' overviews are included in their entirety in both the main text and the study outline

3. The numbered points representing the skeletal outline of the study are extracts from leading sentences to paragraphs in the main text dealing with the detail and substance of the same topic and subtopics

4. The lead paragraphs in the main text form the detail and substance of the corresponding numbered points, topics, subtopics, and sections in the Made For Eternity Study Outline

5. The main text and the study outline are therefore set in a numerical cross reference design to keep you in sync with the main text and the study outline. In order to keep abreast with the outline, simply follow each chapter, topic, subtopic, and section, beginning with the lead numbered paragraphs of the main text and the corresponding numbered points in the study outline

6. At the end of a lesson, or when you elect to pause for questions and discussions, simply use your own method for identifying your stoppage and starting points (Paper clips, sticky papers, penciled notes, or other indicators that you might find useful).

7. The evaluation and discussion questions and their placements are simply the author's suggestions. You may break for questions, group, and/or general discussions at any point of the study to meet the existing teaching and learning demands. You may also add and facilitate questions that may emerge from the learning experience. Additional questions for a comprehensive overview of the study may be found in the appendices.

(My thoughts and prayers are with you as you pursue this worthwhile course of study. I pray that this study experience will strengthen your faith and understanding of the work of the Holy Spirit in the spiritual transformation of your lives. May you truly experience and develop a closer relationship with God as together we encounter Him and come into a better understanding of God's eternal purpose for us. May God through the Lord Jesus in the power of the Holy Spirit guide your steps, inspire your thoughts and renew your minds as you grow in Christ on your journey towards spiritual transformation and ultimately, eternity with God).

2. Introduction/Purpose Statement

The purpose of the book, "Made For Eternity" our main text, which forms the basis of this study outline, was to demonstrate how God uses our faithful participation in worship, mission and eschatological expectations to transform us, aid our growth in Christ and position us for eternity. Christianity is a relationship with Christ that takes us on a faith journey towards spiritual transformation and ultimately glorification. This book is intended to be an Information Model developed as a teaching tool that is aimed at creating a paradigm shift in people's awareness of the means of faith and components of Christianity that engage us the most on our Christian faith journey. These means of faith are worship, Christian mission, and eschatology. This book seeks to demonstrate how God uses our faithful participation in worship, mission and eschatological expectations to transform us, aid our growth in Christ, and position us for eternity. In order to do so, I have set out to examine the relations between the three most prominent components of Christianity and our faith formation that most occupy the Christian's life and practices. These are worship, Christian mission, and eschatology.

These three means of faith are the basic foundational ordinances upon which the process of our spiritual formation and transformation rests. Our participation and engagements in worship, mission and eschatology, are our first steps in a spiritual journey that continues into eternity. It is my intention to help you develop an understanding and appreciation of how the Christian's spiritual life is shaped into holiness as a result of our faithful participation in these means of faith. I also intend to help you understand how we are shaped and empowered by the Holy Spirit to acknowledge and experience God in our daily walk with Christ as we faithfully participate in these means of faith.

These spiritual components or means of faith are participated in and acted upon at different levels of the Christian faith response and journey toward God. As such, they should be understood as foundational means of faith and spiritual formation at three levels. Worship is the level of recognition and formation of divine knowledge and faith. Mission is the level of dedication where faith is practiced and developed. It is also the level where Christian character is formed. Eschatology, by virtue of the promised manifestation of the greater glory and all that this promised glory entails, is the level of ultimate spiritual transformation. It is here that we not only get a glimpse of glory based on the present operation of the Holy Spirit, but also where we hold fast to the promised glory because of the commendable nature of the lifestyle that is inspired and lived in anticipation of the return of Christ.

Through these foundational means of faith, God imparts Himself to us as a relational God through the Son, and sustains that relationship through the gravitating and transforming presence and work of the Holy Spirit. As we faithfully participate in these means of faith, the design of God is to transform and draw us into His divine life through Christ. That way, on every step of our faith journey we are empowered to live and grow into the standard and dignity that God established for us before the foundations of the earth. The spiritually transforming value of worship, mission, and eschatology should therefore not be taken lightly. Indeed, it is our proximity to these means of faith that positions us to hear from, believe in, experience, and therefore hope in God. As we shall see, participating in these means of faith, along with God aiding us by His grace, keeps us in tune with and connected to Christ in whom and through whom we grow in grace and the maturity of God's eternal love.

A good starting point for clarity on the process of our growth is to understand that the Christian life, like the Church, is caught up in a process of existence that begins with our initial knowledge of God. This initial knowledge of God is based fundamentally on the evidence of creation. Our knowledge is then renewed and elevated by the reorientation of our minds, the regeneration of our human attitude and spirit and our reconciliation with God through faith in the person and finished work of the Lord Jesus. This knowledge is then translated and faithfully manifested and sustained in worship. Our knowledge and worship of God are then put into practice through Christian mission where our faith and Christian character are developed. Ultimately, our knowledge, worship, and mission attain their eternal purpose with our realization of the greater glory, which is the theme of eschatology. Put differently, our Christian life journey, which begins with knowledge of God, is nurtured by grace in worship and life. The Christian life is further strengthened and developed through mission as we are sustained by the Holy Spirit. The Holy Spirit then daily reminds us of the promise of eternity, the theme of eschatology, which is the consummation or realization of the greater glory. This consummation is a sort of end product, so to speak, of God's work in us, whereby the believer is spiritually renovated or made new and eternally transformed and fitted for eternity.

I propose then, that these three components of Christianity (worship, mission, and eschatology) are means of faith and the Pillars of Spiritual Transformation. Through these components of Christianity, the truth of faith is set forth, learned, inspired, practiced, and developed by the Holy Spirit that works in us to change us and bring us into conformity to the will and purpose of God. How God applies the Christian's faithful participation in these three components of Christianity for the spiritual development of the Christian's life and faith sets the tone and establishes the backdrop for the development of this book.

I believe it is safe to say that we cannot faithfully and sincerely participate in the things of God without knowing Him and without being transformed by His Holy Spirit to contemplate and pursue the holiness and righteousness of God. Through these three areas of interrelated components of faith and spiritual transformation, God has provided the Holy Spirit to Christian believers as an empowering presence to train us in spiritual things while all the time, engrafting us into Christ. As the Holy Spirit shapes and develops in us those principles and practices that are reflective of the divine holiness of God the Father, we become more like His begotten Son, Jesus, the Christ. Our becoming like Christ is the ultimate goal of spiritual transformation.

As we participate in these means of faith, the Holy Spirit draws us into our life giving center, God, in whom we live, move and have our being. While living and sharing in the life of God may become the Christian's desire, ultimately, the Holy Spirit is the One who shapes and empowers us to exercise holy tempers (attitudes and behaviors) that are reflective of our walk of faith with God. The Holy Spirit shapes us by giving us a clearer, or even better, a new vision of God, while remolding us so that our moral DNA will match the moral attributes of the One in whose image and likeness we were created. As we obediently respond to the divine patterning of the Holy Spirit on our lives, we are transformed into Christ-likeness. That way, we might appropriately live in and reflect the true nature and divine values that God implanted in us in the first place. The Christian life is therefore not a static life, but rather, a dynamic and visional life that changes or is being transformed for the better, so that it might unfold to reveal the beauty that is Christ within us.

Through worship, mission, and eschatological living, God is constantly shaping and reshaping our lives into the fashion of His own likeness. In worship, the Holy Spirit facilitates and lifts our worship to the Son, who, as our High Priest, mediates our worship to the Father. In mission, the Holy Spirit directs our actions. He also sustains and renews our spirit so that what we do in mission may also bring glory to God. As we live eschatologically, with the expectation of Christ returning, the Holy Spirit stirs us to active worship and service and, through grace, keeps us steadfast as He guides us into the promises of eternity with Christ. By virtue of the present work and operations of the Holy Spirit

— XV —

through whom the grace of God is channeled to us, we are in one sense, living in the realization of Christ, while in another sense, we are being moved or carried toward our completion in Christ. This matter of what we have already realized and are still hoping for will be further developed in our discussion on realized yet expected eschatology in chapter seven.

3. The Problem and Basis for the Development of This Resource

The book (main text) from which this study outline is developed This book emerged from the coming together of several strands of projects done as partial fulfillment of the Doctor of Ministry (D. Min.) program at the University of Dubuque Theological Seminary, Dubuque, Iowa, with an emphasis on congregational renewal.

In my first year project, I developed a curriculum that was aimed at assessing and increasing parishioners' awareness of worship. The desire to pursue that line of inquiry came out of discussions during the first year of residency for the D. Min. course of study which carried over into a weekend academic exercise. As a weekend exercise, students were required to attend a worship service of choice in the area. Based on our observations, we were to write a paper reflecting on any existing indicators in the worship service that may have led to an understanding of the relations between the unity of the Father, Son, and Holy Spirit based on the structure, language, and doctrinal formulations of that church's liturgical content.

The content and liturgical execution of the worship service I attended seemed rather self-directed in focus. Based on the theological language and content of the worship service, there did not appear to be any clear understanding of the God-humanward and the human-Godward movement of grace. Indicators of worshippers' understanding, faithful response, and participation were virtually nonexistent. It was as though worshippers were mere observers of prescribed set in stone routines, whereby clergy and lay worship leaders did their thing, as in the performance of a prescribed theatrical role, rather than as faithful respondents and participants in a meaningful encounter with each other and with God. The worship experience was also made to seem like "something we do," rather than what God, through Christ in the power of the Holy Spirit, does in us, for us, and ultimately for God's glory. The "we" element (the Father, Son, Holy Spirit, and the people) of worship was missing. There were no clear connections between the liturgical affirmations and the human real life experiences that are often brought to bear on the worship encounter in the human search for clarity, affirmation, understanding and hope. The worship service was also void of meaningful theological connections between the work of the Father, Son and Holy Spirit for worship as well as for life. An example of theological disconnection was gathered from the message of the day. The message was based on the Genesis account of creation. Notwithstanding that, no reference was made to "the executive arm of God"— the Holy Spirit of God— who was the creative power that "was hovering over the face of the waters." Also, the message made no connection with the work of God in creation and the place, value, and role of humans in relationship with God and as stewards in the advancement of creation. It was a missed opportunity to reaffirm the theological as well as the relational, existential and custodial value that God in creation placed on humanity.

The worship process also came across as being based on repetitive formulations that left worshippers in a state of "what does that mean?" instead of having a clear understanding of the process aided by the liturgical content. That loss of clarity was highlighted by an apparent disconnect between the worship leader and the rest of the congregation. This disconnect was probably due to the absence of any liturgical understanding between the worship leader and the rest of the congregation. The failure to relate the message to the life experiences of those gathered to hear it may have also contributed to that great divide between the speaker and the hearers of the message. I discovered that without that connection, the message remains a mere cognitive feeding without the impetus of passion invoked by the experiential encounters of worshippers with God who kept them throughout the week and brought them to that place of worship for celebration, renewal, and reaffirmation of their dignity and worth. The celebratory aspect of worship was absolutely nonexistent.

I also observed that there was preoccupation with the human performance, which made the worship experience a sort of preconditioned routine rather than an anticipated opportunity to actually experience God. The worship atmosphere and content seemed to imply that this is how "we do worship." This is what our worship service is like. These are the songs that we sing and this is how we sing them. As it relates to the channel of worship— from God, to God, by worshippers, through Christ in the power of the Holy Spirit— no clear understanding was established. Any understanding of the Fatherhood of God, the Sonship and Priesthood of Christ, and the facilitating and sanctifying work of the Holy Spirit during the worship service, was at best, an illusive and disconnected one.

In both practice and doctrine, the worship service lacked any focus on the sole priesthood of Christ. The liturgy itself demonstrated no clear indication of the sanctifying power and presence of the Holy Spirit. Not once was the name of Jesus mentioned and at no time was the Holy Spirit mentioned during the worship service. My concern was that not enough was said or done in the worship service to exalt the unity of the Father, Son and Holy Spirit in whom the fullness of Deity dwells. This type of worship setting according to Torrance is "too often non-sacramental, and can engender weariness."

The immediate realization of the existence of an improper understanding, approach and attitude toward the channel of worship in contemporary Christian worship, led me to pursue an examination of worshippers' perceptions and understanding of worship within the context of the local church where I was the appointed pastor. In all honesty, I was also led to reexamine my own liturgical and pastoral/preaching practices. I was moved by the need for theological depth, clarity, shared spiritual understanding of the worship encounter, the concretization of our faith practices, and a mutually shared worship experience by clergy and laity.

In order to gain knowledge of the extent of the overt and/or covert areas of deficiencies among worshippers concerning worship and liturgical practices in the local setting in which I was embedded, using a Worship, Mission and Eschatology Questionnaire (WMEQ), I set out to examine those worshippers' awareness and perceptions. While there was a relatively reasonable understanding of worship as "homage" and reverence to God, "deficiencies" were found to exist in the overall congregational understanding at three levels. At the first level, deficiencies were found in their overall understanding of God, and the place and role of Christ and the Holy Spirit in the worship encounter. At the second level, there were fundamental deficiencies regarding participants' understanding of liturgical practices and the relations between Christian worship, Christian mission, and eschatology. At the third level, significant deficiencies were identified regarding worshippers' understanding of how our participation in worship, mission, and an eschatological lifestyle spiritually impacts and changes our lives.

Concerned with the adverse impact those deficiencies may have on parishioners' faith formation, intentional participation in the worship process, liturgical understanding, and spiritual transformation, my immediate response was to develop a curriculum with the intention to inform and elevate congregational awareness while addressing and correcting those deficiencies. The curriculum was developed on a sort of tri-level thesis. At the first level, the thrust of the thesis was that increased knowledge of God results in increase participation in worship. At the second level, proper knowledge of God leads to proper worship of God. At the third level, the objective was to demonstrate that understanding of liturgical practices leads to intentional participation, passionate worship, and spiritual transformation. Specifically, the curriculum addressed knowledge of God, worshippers' understanding of God, Christian worship, and the Godward-humanward and the humanward-Godward movements of grace and faith response in worship. The curriculum also included the affirmation of Jesus as our sole intercessor in worship, the Holy Spirit as the facilitator and lifter of our worship, as well as the human response and contribution to worship.

In developing and applying this level of the curriculum, I set out to examine how knowledge of God affects worshippers' understanding and attitude toward worship. The content of the curriculum was also incorporated with sermons that were shared with the entire congregation over a six month period nestled in a teaching paradigm. The objective was to elevate and nurture mutual awareness while developing a common consensus and understanding of the worship and liturgical processes.

Having developed the curriculum, a Focus Group was established within the local ministry setting to be a resource team for the four year duration of the D. Min. program. The Focus Group was made up of adults and teenage members of the Sunday school and Bible study classes. Although the project was set in a didactic paradigm designed to appeal to and elevate participants' cognition, it also included opportunities for experiential sharing, meaningful participation, and open discussions of the subject areas presented. A detailed outline of the implementation (methodology) of the study can be found in Appendix 1.

I was satisfied with the results of the study. The Focus Group's final evaluation of the study also shows significant advancements in their understanding when measured against where they had begun. My satisfaction was further enhanced as I witnessed the intentional participation, sense making, and practical application of the learning processes as manifested through conversations and the ensuing worship experiences. These, altogether, translated into higher levels of passionate worship. The thesis that increased knowledge results in increase participation, that proper knowledge leads to proper worship, and that understanding leads to passionate worship participation, was affirmed.

The second year project focused on Christian mission and the relations between Christian worship and mission. The third year project was a critical content analysis of eschatology and the importance of eschatology for our spiritual formation, transformation, and growth in Christ. The development, advancement, and weaving together of the components of worship, mission, and eschatology came in the final year of D. Min course of study. The original study for the fulfilment of the D. Min. program was about 165 pages. That study has since been vastly expanded to become what is now this book.

My effort was to help worshippers (parishioners) understand, through a teaching format, how the Christian's life is a continuous process of participation that finds expression through knowledge of God, our faithful participation in worship, mission, and an eschatological lifestyle. How that participation impacts Christians' spiritual growth, as the Holy Spirit transforms our lives and engrafts us in Christ, formed the platform for that project and now saturates the content of this book/study outline.

4. What You Will Find in this Book/Study Outline

This book is not a self-help book. It is not another step-by-step how to claim it and receive it get-rich formula. This book is about worship, Christian mission, and eschatology. It is a Spirit-driven attempt to glorify God in its content, witness, and experiential affirmations. This resource is expressly designed to direct people toward God through their faith response to Christ and their faithful participation in those means of faith formation (worship, Christian mission, and eschatology), which God uses to develop godly characters and therefore Christ-mindedness in us.

Though this book is grounded in an informative paradigm, it is a practical coming together of information, Christian experience, personal witness, exhortation, and the affirmation of hope. The issues raised and the discussions lifted up in the content of this book are not limited to academic interests and theological discussions or argumentations. They are of relevant and practical spiritual value and significance based on sound biblical applications, testimonies and experiences of God's outworking grace and favor.

This resource is an intentional attempt to concretize our theological understanding by the development of a systematic synthesis of the three components of the Christian faith— worship, mission and eschatology— that are grounded in the human experience. The objective is to give feet to our faith, hands to the gift of grace, and understanding and sense making to our participation in these components of faith that most occupy our time and thinking.

The goal is to remove the myth, the mystical, and the abstract, and bring the process of our faith response to God, our faithful participation in the components of the Christian faith, and the operation of the Holy Spirit into the existential (the realm of human existence). That way, we can see, experience, and understand how God, through Christ, in the presence and power of the Holy Spirit, accompanies Christian believers in all areas of their lives in order that He might spiritually transform, accumulatively nurture, refashion us into His own likeness, and ready us for eternity.

As such, I hope that this resource will help you understand more clearly this process of spiritual transformation. I also hope to help you come to grips with what will eternally become of all the things we participate in as Christians and people of faith.

This book will help you understand through scripture, that you were made for eternity and how intent God is on sharing His eternity with you. You will develop a sense of how intent God is on saving and transforming your life in readiness for eternity with the knowledge that eternity with God has always been a predisposed preference established by God for us, before the foundations of the earth.

This book is built on the premise that knowledge of God, worship, mission, and eschatology are the foundational pillars and means of faith that God uses for our spiritual formation and renewal and our becoming all that we can be in Christ. Worship, mission, and eschatology are therefore not three separate components of Christian practices. They are one continuously interlocking process that engulfs our spiritual transformation.

This book posits that if, indeed, worship is the spiritual encounter, then mission, must necessarily lead to the spiritual formation and development of the Christian life and character through service and self-giving love. Eschatologically, as we continuously share in the Holy Spirit's gift of mission to the world, we are kept diligent because of our expectation of Christ's returning. Worship, liturgical practices, and life experiences are our training models for knowing God. Christian mission in the world is the training ground for the formation of Christian character and the place where the seeds planted in worship grow into fuller blooms of the knowledge of God.

As we shall see later, our eschatological expectations, based on the promises of Christ to return, invoke a lifestyle that orients us toward the future. However, in the present, those eschatological expectations also keep us grounded in holiness and instill within us the desire to faithfully worship God. In turn, this invokes in us an awesome sense of responsibility that leads us to service and the making of disciples for Christ.

It is my goal to use this medium to transform the way we think about worship while inspiring our faithful participation in worship. It is also my intention to help you, the reader, discover information that will help you develop a clearer understanding of God, what worship is, the purposes of liturgical practices, your role as an active and participative worshipper, the Priesthood of Christ, and the role of the Holy Spirit in our worship encounters and missional pursuits.

Throughout the pages of this book, you will receive information that will help you concretize your understanding and experience as they relate to your faithful participation in the worship and mission of Jesus, the Son, to God, the Father. This information will transform the way you think about worship and Christian mission because it will take you beyond yourself and what you do in worship and mission to focus on Christ and what He has already accomplished. You will be empowered to see that worship and mission are not distinct components that separately impact the Christian's life. Rather, they are combined and continuous processes whereby the faith we confess in formal worship becomes the practical manifestation of our faith through mission and our service to God in the world.

This book is therefore designed to assist and nurture your understanding of the relations between the formal Sunday worship and everyday Christian life and mission. You will become inspired by the realization that Christian mission is in fact, a practical living out of the formal worship and a way of presenting and glorifying God in the world.

You will be presented with a fresh look at eschatology that will help you develop an understanding concerning the nearness of God and how that nearness is a daily challenge as well as an opportunity for you to respond to that nearness with faith and obedience. As you live in the anticipated fulfillment of God's promise of eternity for you, which is the eschatological lifestyle I speak of, you will be challenged to exercise diligence in your worship of God and your service to others inspired by this lifestyle that is lived in readiness for Christ's reappearing.

Guided by biblical and sound theological persuasions, this book promotes the conviction that our encounter with the Lord does not only lead to personal faith renewal and holiness. That encounter also comes with a faith response which leads to an assignment and a responsibility. You shall see then, that in this book, theology and faith talks are not merely theological ramblings. Such discourses are convictions and declarations of faith in the God whom we seek to know, worship, understand, trust, and intentionally serve. The purpose of faith is to connect us with God as well as to nurture belief in God who infinitely loves us. The purpose of faith is also to change one's attitude and inspire a Christian lifestyle that is pleasing and acceptable to God. This lifestyle is the manifestation of our changed lives because of what we know and believe about God and have become in Christ Jesus. Certainly, faith not only encourages belief; faith is also manifested behavior and demonstrative service. This is precisely what James meant when he said, "…Faith by itself, if it does not have works, is dead."[1]

We shall see that while faith encourages belief and finds genuine expression through our intentional participation in the ministry of Christ to God the Father, it is also the impetus for our service to God in the world. An encounter with God is therefore an opportunity as well as a privilege to honor and bow down to worship God. At the same time, as we shall see, our encounter with God is a commission, and therefore a responsibility to go out on assignment to serve God in the world. While some of us may claim to possess great faith, or even a little, as if it were a privilege, faith is not a

---

[1] Jas 2:17

privilege. Faith is a gift of grace. As such, faith becomes our active response to God through obedience, and our duty to our neighbor through loving service. Our active faith response to God and the good works we exercise on behalf of our neighbor, make faith practical, and keep faith alive and working because faith without works is dead. Faith that transforms is faith that is alive and working to give God glory while moving us to use our active faith to change the human condition.

In this book, you will also discover a multitude of easy in-text and footnote scriptural references to inspire and guide you in your reading and daily study.

Also, at the beginning of each chapter, you will find selected and inspiring prayers, suggested scripture readings, and hymns to encourage and guide your devotional lifestyle. My prayer is that the God of grace will be with you in your study, worship and service, to enlighten, transform, strengthen, guide, renew, and empower you.

If such pursuits and understanding are of value for you in your personal search for understanding and spiritual and theological clarity, or for application in your congregational settings, and I suspect that they are, then the content of this book and the Made For Eternity Study Outline that accompanies this resource will be of tremendous value to such pursuits and understanding.

Having issues with forgiveness? There is a section on forgiveness tailor-made for you. Struggling with sin and your growth in Christ? Check out chapter four, section C: "Baptism: An Opportunity to Grow in Grace." Here you will see that it takes time to grow in Christ and that you have His help to do so. Do you have a desire to know Jesus better? Read chapter nine, "One Final Question: Do you know Jesus?" Do you need to understand why God does the things He does for us? Read chapter eight, "Motivated and Transformed by Love."

Come with me! This is going to be a spiritually transforming ride that takes us to new levels of understanding of the means of faith that we participate in as Christians, and the way God uses our faithful participation in these means of faith to transform us and position us for eternity.

CHAPTER ONE

YOU WERE MADE FOR ETERNITY

Devotional Exercise
> Welcome/Greetings
> Sharing of prayer concerns
> Prayer
> Hymn(s) of the day
> Scripture selection(s) for today

Prayer:

Dear God, I give my life to You. By faith, I make You the God and Savior of my soul. I believe that Jesus, begotten of You before there was time, died for me. Let Your Holy Spirit take control of my mind, my thoughts, my actions, and all of my ways. Complete me with Your love and grace. Keep me steadfast, intentional, and faithful as I continue to worship and serve You in anticipation of the return of Christ. Ready me for Your eternity by instilling in me the spirit of faith and obedience. I give You the glory and the praise for all that You are, all that You have done, and all that You have promised to do. In the precious name of Jesus I pray, Amen!

Suggested Scripture Readings: Jn. 5:24, 6:39, 17:2; 1 Jn. 3: 2, 5: 11, 13; Rom. 8:18-19, 29-30; Tit. 1:2 Jude 21; Gal. 5: 22-26; Col. 3: 9-10; Heb. 10: 1-18

Hymns:
> "All to Jesus I Surrender"
> "Lord Jesus, I Long To Be Perfectly Whole"
> "O, They Told Me of A Home"

Objective
To aid us in understanding:

- God's interest and pursuit of us
- How intent God is in redeeming and restoring our relationship with Him
- How we were created with the moral and divine DNA of God
- How eternity with God is a predisposed preference for our pursuit implanted in each of us by God

- How our journey towards God begins with God and will ultimately find fulfillment/culmination in Him
- Of how we, finite creatures of time, restricted by and living in time, have the affinity to yearn for the Creator and the infinite by virtue of God's divine implantation in us

1. YOU WERE MADE FOR ETERNITY
(SECTION ONE)

1. You were made for eternity!

2. The truth is, when we are far away from God, God misses us far more than we miss Him

3. The Bible further indicates in Ephesians 2: 4-5 that "God is rich in mercy and because of His great love with which He loves us, even when we were dead in trespasses He made us alive together with Christ

4. Hell was not prepared for you

5. Notwithstanding that however, do not become overly preoccupied with hellfire and brimstone and the massive unending burning lake

6. You were not made for a place like that (hell)

7. Our journey towards God begins with God

8. God, as we shall see later, is a communal God who lives in fellowship with Jesus the Son and the Holy Spirit

9. God placed eternity in our hearts so that we would not become satisfied with and therefore surrender to the mundane and unworthy pursuits which are also prisoners of time

10. Eternity with God is therefore a predisposed preference for our pursuit implanted in each of us by God

11. We are creatures of time destined for eternity

12. This finite grasping for the infinite is God's blueprint in us that motivates and inspires us to follow His design for our growth and development in Him

13. The Eternal God has, by the act of His own will, created and brought into existence from nothingness, all things that were not but now are

14. Furthermore, if we conclude that human existence encompasses the respective dimensions of the past, present, and future, we would be remiss had we not also concluded that it is the coming together of these three dimensions which completes human existence and selfhood

15. Our infinite God puts humans in time and places temporality (the limitation of space and time) upon us so that we have the time we need to develop knowledge of God and learn of His will and divine nature

16. God, as the essence of Being, embodies time and eternity

17. With the end of time, all things are gathered up in God who has been their Source in the first place

—

PAUSE FOR REVIEW
SEE QUESTIONS BELOW TO HELP GUIDE YOUR DISCUSSIONS. YOU MAY
ADD YOUR OWN QUESTIONS THAT MAY HAVE COME OUT OF YOUR STUDY
EXPERIENCE TOGETHER

EVALUATION/DISCUSSION QUESTION

1. What do you think is implied by the statement "you were made for eternity?"

2. Why do you think God is interested in us?

3. How do you feel about God's interest in and pursuit of you?

4. "Hell was not prepared for you." Discuss this statement with scriptural support

5. Time is our friend. Using today's lesson, explain the benefit of time to our spiritual development and preparation for eternity

YOU WERE MADE FOR ETERNITY
(SECTION TWO)

1. Since we were not created to find fulfillment in ourselves, but rather, in God, eternity and the realization of our greater potential, our transformation into the glory of Christ and therefore the holiness of God, must be God's ultimate design for us

2. This Christhood or Christ-likeness, toward which we are progressively being drawn by the Holy Spirit at work in us, is the culmination of God's purpose for those who recognize His nearness in Christ and believe Him for salvation

3.   Through creation, God conferred Himself on us and fit us, in time, with the capacity for a virtuous living that prepares us for eternity

4.   For the time being, let us go back to the matter of our being made for eternity

5.   Since all things created come from God, it follows that the moral and divine fiber, the very DNA of God, is intertwined in our humanity

6.   Notwithstanding our shortcomings and failures, God loves us

7.   In Christ we have redemption and forgiveness according to the riches of His grace

8.   Because of this anticipation of glory, this promise of eternity with God, inspired by the present manifestation of God's love for us, we are motivated to continuously love, worship, and serve God in time and space

9.   As we have already established, the three components or areas of participation and opportunity for fellowship with God on our faith journey are worship, Christian mission, and an eschatological lifestyle that is inspired by our expectation of Christ's return

10. Through worship, mission, and eschatological living, God is constantly shaping and reshaping our lives into the fashion of His own likeness and holy standards

11. Through the Holy Spirit, then, we live in the realization of Christ and yet are being moved or carried toward our completion in Christ through grace

12. It may be useful to point out at this juncture that eternity is not a place

13. According to Jesus in John 17:3, we have eternal life the moment our minds are reoriented to God through knowledge that transforms, and the very moment that we believe in Christ and turn to God through Him in repentance and faith[2]

PAUSE FOR REVIEW

SEE QUESTIONS BELOW TO HELP GUIDE YOUR DISCUSSIONS. YOU MAY ADD YOUR OWN QUESTIONS THAT MAY HAVE COME OUT OF YOUR STUDY EXPERIENCE TOGETHER

EVALUATION/DISCUSSION QUESTIONS

1. **What and who do you think are the basis for human fulfillment?**

2. **What do you think it means to be engrafted in Christ? Give examples**

3. **What do you think is meant by the statement, "We were made with the fiber of the eternal God?"**

4. **Why do you think God is so intent to redeem fallen humanity?**

5. **What are the means used by God to sustain a spiritual and life transforming relationship with us?**

---

[2] Jn 3:16, 18; 5:24; 6:47

CHAPTER TWO

SPIRITUAL TRANSFORMATION

Devotional Exercise

    Welcome/Greetings
    Sharing of prayer concerns
    Prayer
    Hymn(s) of the day
    Scripture Selection(s) for today

Prayer:

    Most holy and eternal God, take hold of us and transform us by the power of Your Holy Spirit so that we may be renewed in our minds. Help us we pray, to reflect the newness we have found in Christ Jesus by the way we walk before You in obedience and faith and the way that we behave toward others. This we pray in the redeeming name of Jesus. Amen!

Scriptures:

    Ps 51:10; Isa 40:31; Rom 12:2; 2 Cor 3:18, 4:16, 5:16-17; Eph 4:23, 5: 8-9; Col 3:10; Tit 3:5; 1 Pet 1:14-15

Hymns:

    "Breathe On Me Breath Of God"
    "This Is The Day Of New Beginnings"
    "Spirit Of The Living God"
    "Something Beautiful"
    "Nothing But The Blood"
    "I Know It Was The Blood"

Objectives
To help us:

- Understand how God works in our lives through the present operations of the Holy Spirit to renew our minds, change our attitude, and bring us into conformity with His holiness and eternal purpose
- Develop an understanding of the process of spiritual transformation

1. OVERVIEW
WHAT IS SPIRITUAL TRANSFORMATION?

What God is seeking to do through the process of spiritual transformation is to infuse His Spirit in us and with our human spirit. That way, He can gracefully and progressively override our human tendencies and develop in us the affinity to become like Him and so reflect Him in the world.

A word about what it means to be spiritual may be helpful in furthering our understanding of this segment of our study as well as the ensuing and prevailing theme that runs throughout the pages of this book. Being spiritual has to do with a mindset that is oriented toward God. That is why any relationship with God and any understanding of the ways of God must necessarily begin with a renewing of the mind. To be spiritual is to be liberated from the limitation of individualism and self-centeredness. Being spiritual implies that our focus is shifted from the natural human inclinations, to embrace the will and purposes of God. To be spiritual is to exercise mastery of self or our natural human tendencies while allowing the Spirit of God to exercise control over us. Being spiritual is therefore a striving toward, a submission to, as well as a connection with a higher power, God! To be spiritual also has to do with the demonstration of faith, obedience, love, justice, mercy, truthfulness, positive thinking, peace, kindness and joy, within the framework of our day-to-day activities. These are outpouring manifestations of the Spirit's presence in the believers' lives as the Spirit of God works in us to transform us.

Now, then, spiritual transformation is the result of change that has taken place in someone's thinking, behavior and attitude. The spiritually transformed person is therefore a person who has been radically changed to respond to God with a renewed mind that is fixed on God, who is essentially our divine center and activity. Spiritual transformation is followed by our willingness to follow the indicative faith statements of the Gospel of Christ, as we intentionally seek to live that Gospel's imperatives in the world for the expressed purpose of glorifying God. Spiritual transformation is a process of renewal in the Christian's attitude and behavior.

Spiritual transformation begins with a renewed mind and therefore a new perspective of one's self in relation to God. Spiritual transformation is the reorientation or the redirection of the believer's mind toward things that pertain to divine values and purpose. The mind that is spiritually renewed is the mind that is turned toward Christ whom we confess and accept as Lord and Savior. The transformed life is the sanctified and liberated life that is lived in Christ and under the authority of the Holy Spirit. To be spiritually transformed is to be renewed and empowered or anointed to live the Christian life through faith that honors and pleases God, having been set free from the limitations of individualism and the bondage of self and sin. By extension, the transformed life is the life that follows the indicative faith statements of the Gospel of Christ. It is also the life that embodies the Gospel's imperatives to walk in faith, obedience, and holiness before God, as well as to serve and do the will of God as we are empowered by the Holy Spirit of grace to do so.

—

PAUSE FOR REVIEW
QUESTIONS/COMMENTS/CLARIFICATIONS
BREAK INTO GROUP DISCUSSIONS

2. SPIRITUAL TRANSFORMATION IS THE WORK OF THE HOLY SPIRIT

1. The work of spiritual transformation is the work of the Holy Spirit

2. As we continue to worship, witness through mission, and live in eschatological hope of Christ returning, our strength, boldness, and hope in the promise of Christ, are renewed in us by the Holy Spirit who indwells us

3. Spiritual transformation is therefore marked by the extent of affinity in the relationship between the Spirit of God and the human spirit

—

PAUSE FOR LESSON REVIEW
QUESTIONS/COMMENTS/CLARIFICATIONS
BREAK INTO GROUP DISCUSSIONS

EVALUATION/DISCUSSION QUESTIONS

1. **What do you think spiritual transformation is?**

2. **What do you think it means to be spiritual? Can you give some examples?**

3. **What do you think are some of the indicators of change or spiritual transformation in a person?**

4. **Please share with us your assessment of your own spiritual transformation**

5. **Share with us your understanding of how the Holy Spirit works in our lives to transform us**

3. SIX STEPS FOR UNDERSTANDING SPIRITUAL TRANSFORMATION

There are six steps in the process of spiritual transformation. These are: (1) Recognizing and knowing God (2) Repentance (3) Forgiveness (4) Justification (5) Sanctification and (6) Moving from glory to glory.

A. Step One: Recognizing and Knowing God

1. The first step in the process of spiritual transformation is to recognize and know God; who God is and what He has done for us in Christ Jesus

2. The greatest gift one can receive is the gift of knowing God because, knowing God as Jesus indicates, is eternal life[3]

3. To better understand the fundamental principles of knowing God, the following questions may be useful in guiding our discussion:
   (a) What are the ways by which we may have knowledge of God?
   (b) How can we get to know God relationally and how does that knowledge change us?
   (c) How is knowledge of God the basis for human excellence?

4. The first question for aiding our understanding of the principle of knowing God is "What are the ways by which we may know God?" We can develop knowledge of God in five mutually inclusive ways. These are:

   (i) **Knowing God by His divine qualities and works (through Creation, Redemption, and Incarnation)**

   (ii) **Knowing God Through God's Own Self-revelation**

   (iii) **Knowing God Through Studying His Word**

   (iv) **Knowing God Intellectually**

   (v) **Knowing God Experientially**

   Let us examine these separately.

---

[3] John 17: 3

(i) Knowing God by His divine qualities and works
(Through Creation, Redemption, and Incarnation)

1. The first way by which we know God is by His divine qualities and works as evidenced in history through creation, incarnation, redemption through Christ, and His continuous work of restoration and sanctification through the Holy Spirit

2. The Psalmist is not at all presumptuous when he affirms that only a fool after observing the order and beauty of creation, and after recognizing his/her own existence, can say in the heart that there is no God[4]

3. Through the incarnation of Christ, God came to us as Redeemer

4. To illustrate the point about the invisible presence being manifested in the world and the human experience, I recall a story about a woman who worked really hard to send her son through school and later to college

5. Later that night they both went to bed

6. The God we worship may indeed be a mystery; but He is not a myth nor is He a human construct or a figment of the human imagination

(ii) Knowing God Through God's Own Self-Revelation

1. The second way for getting to know God is by God's own self-revelation

2. The human intellect is incapable of knowing God without God's help

---

[4] Ps 14:1

3.   Since knowledge of God comes to us from God's own self-revelation, God is therefore the centrality of revelation and the Source of human wisdom

4.   Indeed, by our intentional faith response to the prompting of the Holy Spirit to contemplate God, we develop new knowledge of ourselves

5.   By virtue of God's self-revelation, and as a direct result of the Holy Spirit stirring up within us thoughts of God, we are moved to pursue knowledge of God[5]

(iii) Knowing God by Studying His Word

1.   The third way by which we can get to know God is by studying His Word, the Bible

2.   As we are led to capture the true spirit of the Word, what we understand and proceed to teach, becomes a matter of divine influence orchestrated by God through the working of His Holy Spirit[6]

3.   Studying and living by the Word are important to Christian formation and subsequent transformation

4.   The Word of God is our sword for Christian witness and warfare[7]

(iv) Knowing God Intellectually

1.   The fourth way by which we get to know God is by our intellect

---

[5] Hos 6: 3; Acts 17:27

[6] 1 Cor 2:13

[7] Eph 6:17; Heb 4:12

2. Christian excellence, transformation, and spiritual maturation are therefore the results of both grace through faith and a rehabilitation of the human mind and way of thinking

3. Regarding intellectual knowledge of God and our growth into that knowledge and understand, Charry observes that two requirements for progress in the Christian life immediately present themselves

4. Intellectual knowledge by itself cannot change us

5. When we speak in theological or spiritual discourses of the human heart, we are not speaking of that muscular pulsating organ in the chest cavity that uses rhythmic and contracting forces to pump blood in order to supply and maintain the circulatory system

6. God is seeking to influence the human heart for three reasons

7. Contrary to popular opinion, it is not the human will that influences our faith, heart response, or holy actions toward God

8. In order to transform us and set us on our way to eternity then, God moves us at four levels

9. Intellectual awareness may begin the process but we need to apply our faith and heart so that we may both know and experience God as Creator and Redeemer

(v) Knowing God Experientially

1. The fifth way for developing knowledge of God is through our experience of God in our personal lives. This is known as experiential knowledge of God. There are many ways by which we may experience God in our personal lives

2. Knowing God experientially also has to do with someone having the recognition or the acknowledgment of God accompanied by a demonstrative faith response to God

3. Knowing God experientially and therefore personally, means that God plays a significant part in your life, in your thinking, in your planning, and in the way you conduct yourself

4. Let us now address the second question for guiding our understanding of the fundamental principles of knowing God, "How can we get to know God relationally and how does that knowledge change us?"

5. As we come to relationally know God through Jesus Christ and become acquainted with what He has done for us through the finished work of Christ, that knowledge renews us

6. The third question that may guide our understanding of the fundamental principles of knowing God is "How is knowledge of God the basis for human excellence?"

7. Human excellence is developed when we know God as:

8. After all, while it is the Christian hope to live eternally, we are not called to wait to be like God in the life after the resurrection

9. We cannot say we know and love God when our lives are not guided by those moral attributes and principles that emanate from God

10. When we know God as holy, something of the holiness of God must rub off on us

11. Knowledge of God leads to a new identity of ourselves in relationship to God

12. At no stage of our faith journey do we come to a state of moral goodness by our own merit

13. Knowledge of God not only awakens our awareness of God's existence, such knowledge revealed by God alone, is also intended to grab us at the very core of our being, and redirect our minds, attitudes, and behaviors toward God

14. Why then does God want us to "find" Him and therefore know Him?

———

PAUSE FOR REVIEW

SEE QUESTIONS BELOW TO HELP GUIDE YOUR DISCUSSIONS. YOU MAY ADD YOUR OWN QUESTIONS THAT MAY HAVE COME OUT OF YOUR STUDY EXPERIENCE TOGETHER

EVALUATION/DISCUSSION QUESTIONS

1. **Why is knowledge of God important for our spiritual transformation?**

2. **Share with us some of the ways that you have personally come to know God**

3. **Knowing God inspires human excellence. Do you agree? If yes, how?**

4. **"When we know God, something of the holiness of God must rub off on us." How would you explain this statement?**

5. **How do you think knowledge of God can help us understand our own identity and relationship with God?**

Having looked at knowledge as the first step in the process of spiritual transformation, let us now turn our attention to the second step, repentance.

B. Step Two: Repentance

1. The second step in the process of spiritual transformation is repentance

2. It is God that gives us knowledge and awareness of Himself as well as awareness of our own moral state of existence. This awareness moves us to seek after God through repentance

3. It is also God that moves us to come to Him in repentance

———

PAUSE FOR REVIEW

SEE QUESTIONS BELOW TO HELP GUIDE YOUR DISCUSSIONS. YOU MAY
ADD YOUR OWN QUESTIONS THAT MAY HAVE COME OUT OF YOUR STUDY
EXPERIENCE TOGETHER

EVALUATION/DISCUSSION QUESTIONS

1. **Why do you think repentance is important in the process of spiritual transformation?**

2. In your own words, please explain how knowledge of God leads us to repentance

3. If God does not move us to repentance, would we ever repent?

C. Step Three: Forgiveness
(Section One)
(Give It If You Want To Receive It— Matthew 6:14-16)

1. Forgiveness is a fundamental principle for Christian living and freedom yet it is one of the things holding many of us in bondage today

2. During the course of this discussion on forgiveness, I will attempt to answer the following questions and in the process find out what the Bible says about forgiveness:

3. What is forgiveness?

4. Forgiveness is not pretending as though nothing was wrong, that no offense was committed, and that no one was hurt

5. Forgiveness is not conditional

6. Forgiveness is not weakness

7. Forgiveness is not to be partially given

8. Forgiveness does not mean that we have lost

9. Let us look at five (5) mutually inclusive keys to walking in forgiveness— Keys to forgiveness number one: We need to accept forgiveness as a command and not as a suggestion

10. When Jesus says get up from the altar and go and make things right with our brother or sister with whom there is an offense, does that mean that we are responsible for someone else's offensive behavior and grudges against us?

11. We may also gather from this statement by Jesus that sometimes people will hold something against you when they should not

12. Keys to forgiveness number two: There is no limit to forgiveness

13. Key to forgiveness number three: Unforgiveness holds us in bondage

14. Unforgiveness holds us in bondage because it can limit or even cut off the blessings of God for our life

15. Keys to forgiveness number four: Forgiveness is a choice

16. Keys to forgiveness number five: Forgiveness leads to reconciliation

17. Why should we forgive those who offend us?

———

PAUSE FOR REVIEW

SEE QUESTIONS BELOW TO HELP GUIDE YOUR DISCUSSIONS. YOU MAY
ADD YOUR OWN QUESTIONS THAT MAY HAVE COME OUT OF YOUR STUDY
EXPERIENCE TOGETHER

EVALUATION/DISCUSSION QUESTIONS

1. Why do you think forgiving others is so difficult for most people including Christians?

2. When and how do we know that forgiveness has taken place?

3. Sometimes God forgives us but we have a hard time forgiving ourselves. Why do you think this happens?

Forgiveness
(Section Two)
(It is Freedom from Bondage— Ephesians 4: 32; Colossians 3: 12-14)

1. The absence of forgiveness in a person's life is a destructive bondage that causes strife, division, depression, oppression, sickness, and broken relationships including marriage and divorce

2. If forgiveness is to take place and our freedom from sin and human offenses obtained, we should not wait for someone to apologize

3. Forgiveness does not mean that our sins or offenses have been overlooked or lightly dismissed

4. It should be noted that when we forgive someone who has done us wrong we cannot remit or get rid of that person's sin

5. Is it okay to feel anger and to desire justice from the person who has offended us?

6. From a human perspective, forgiveness does not mean that we are suddenly bosom buddies with those who have offended us

7. Forgiveness compels us to let go of our pride

8. So then, is forgiveness a conscious choice, or an emotional response?

9. How should we forgive and should we forgive even when we do not feel like it?

10. We should forgive just as God forgives

11. What then is forgiveness?

12. Because sin is burdensome, by His mercy, God releases us of it so that we may be elevated to new levels of awareness concerning His holiness as well as to new levels of relationship with Christ

13. By what means are we forgiven?

14. How do we know that forgiveness has taken place?

15. Who then, should take the initiative in forgiveness?

16. Learning how to forgive others is one of the most unnatural duties in the Christian life.

17. Forgiveness is freedom from bondage

18. Forgiveness is freedom from turmoil and the freedom to live in peace and walk in the holiness of God

19. Forgiveness sets us free

—

| PAUSE FOR LESSON REVIEW |
| QUESTIONS/COMMENTS/CLARIFICATIONS |
| BREAK INTO GROUP DISCUSSIONS |

EVALUATION/DISCUSSION QUESTIONS

1. **Do you think forgiving others should be based on how we feel or should it be a moral obligation to forgive?**

2. **What do you think it means to forgive just as God forgives?**

3. **Do you think it is reasonable to expect God to forgive us when we are not willing to forgive others who may have offended us?**

Forgiveness
(Section Three)
(God's Benevolent Fixing Of Us— Psalm 51)

1. Psalm 51 is a great example of the repentant cry of a broken person and that person's appeal to the benevolence of God

2. This psalm gives us an inside view of the mind of the repentant sinner

3. When we realize that we have sinned, we have a choice

4. Sin is transgression

5. Sin is iniquity

6. When we give ourselves over to a sinful lifestyle, we are committing iniquity because by giving way to a lifestyle of sin, sin has become our master (Romans 6:14)

7. Forgiveness requires that we forgive just as God in Christ has forgiven us

8. Forgiveness is not something we earn

9. As a gift from God, forgiveness puts us in a position of trust and obedience to God

10. Humans may or may not show mercy but because of His benevolent grace, God is merciful

11. When trouble surrounds you, and you need to be delivered, place yourself in the hand of God because your deliverance depends on whose hands you are in

12. When I am in trouble, I would rather be put in the hand of God for judgment than be in the human hands

13. When we go to God for forgiveness, we do so because we believe and act under the conviction and assurance that God is love

14. God's benevolence is nondiscriminatory

15. Because of God's benevolent fixing of us, the joy of our salvation is restored

16. We have sinned against God and each other; and God alone by His benevolent favor has forgiven and redeemed us through Christ

17. By His benevolent grace, God alone has established us in Christ

18. Justice demanded that we should die

—

PAUSE FOR REVIEW

SEE QUESTIONS BELOW TO HELP GUIDE YOUR DISCUSSIONS. YOU MAY ADD YOUR OWN QUESTIONS THAT MAY HAVE COME OUT OF YOUR STUDY EXPERIENCE TOGETHER

EVALUATION/DISCUSSION QUESTIONS

1. **Based on Psalm 51, in what ways is sin a transgression that may lead to iniquity?**

2. "Forgiveness is not something that we earn." Explain.

3. Explain why you would rather be judged by God rather than your peers

4. How would explain the statement that God is a benevolent God?

5. What does it really mean to be Christians?

6. Justice demanded that we should die; but grace and mercy say, "Oh no we have already paid the price." Please take a moment to share with each other your understanding of this statement

Forgiveness
(Section Four)
(Forgiven People Are Changed People—2 Cor. 5: 17-21)

1. God forgives us in order to change the downward spiraling of our lives

2. We cannot therefore say that we have been forgiven and changed when we do not demonstrate the evidences of having been forgiven and changed

3. We cannot say that we have repented, are forgiven, changed, saved, and are indeed Christians just because we think we are good persons

4. We are not Christians because we have lifelong church memberships

5. The person and the church that have been forgiven and renewed become part and parcel of a community and fellowship where there is holiness and goodwill towards each other

6. The new life in Christ means that we must leave our old self with all of its old unchristian behaviors and our old baggage of sin behind

7. Through forgiveness, with the Holy Spirit reorienting of our minds toward God, and infusing us with new thoughts, we begin to progressively display the emergence of new attitudes so that even our behavior is changed to act toward God

8. The question that confronts us and needs to be answered at this juncture is, "Why are we changed?"

—

PAUSE FOR REVIEW
SEE QUESTIONS BELOW TO HELP GUIDE YOUR DISCUSSIONS. YOU MAY ADD YOUR OWN QUESTIONS THAT MAY HAVE COME OUT OF YOUR STUDY EXPERIENCE TOGETHER

EVALUATION/DISCUSSION QUESTIONS

1. **In what ways should forgiveness be reflected in our behavior?**

2. **What does it really mean to be Christians?**

3. **Why do you think God changes us and are these changes sudden or progressive?**

4. **Please take a moment to share with each other how you think the Holy Spirit works in us to make forgiveness practically displayed?**

D. Step Four: Justification

1. When someone is justified it means that the person's relationship with God has been made right and the person declared innocent

2. Justification is part of God's plan of salvation

3. Justification is God removing our guilt and sinfulness and giving us a new start

---

PAUSE FOR LESSON REVIEW
QUESTIONS/COMMENTS/CLARIFICATIONS
BREAK INTO GROUP DISCUSSIONS

EVALUATION/DISCUSSION QUESTIONS

1. **What is your understanding of justification?**

2. **Do you think we are deserving of justification? If yes or no, why or why not?**

3. **Share with us your understanding of justification by grace through faith**

E. Step Five: Sanctification

1. The fifth step in the process of spiritual transformation takes place at the level of sanctification by the Holy Spirit

2. Sanctification is the work of God who enters humans' lives and experiences to change us and set us apart from

3. Sanctification is the work of God who enters humans' lives and experiences to change us and set us apart from unprofitable pursuits

4. The question that confronts us and needs to be answered at this juncture is, "Why are we changed and set apart (sanctified)?" A litany of affirmations, which is by no means exclusive, would be appropriate here. Let us consider them: *(Present list of reasons why we are changed and set apart as outlined in main text)*

—

PAUSE FOR REVIEW
SEE QUESTIONS BELOW TO HELP GUIDE YOUR DISCUSSIONS. YOU MAY ADD YOUR OWN QUESTIONS THAT MAY HAVE COME OUT OF YOUR STUDY EXPERIENCE TOGETHER

EVALUATION/DISCUSSION QUESTIONS

1. **When it comes to sanctification, what is it that God is calling to and setting us apart from?**

2. **If sanctification is God's design used to develop godly lifestyles in us, what do you think is the importance of a godly lifestyle?**

3. **List three changes that you have experienced in your life since you have accepted Jesus as Savior and Lord**

F. Step Six: Moving From Glory to Glory
(Section One)

1. Moving from glory to glory is indicative of our progressive spiritual ascension to the ultimate level of spiritual transformation

2. The Bible tells us that human's glory comes from God and is given or bestowed by God (1 Chron 29:12; Ps 3:3), but it cannot be shared

3. When we speak of God's glory, we are speaking of His divine esteem so to speak

4. The New Testament also speaks of another unveiling of God's glory

5. Furthermore, while the common glory of human achievements is subjective and often ascribed glory, the glory of God is not subjective but objective

6. Now then, our moving from glory to glory is therefore indicative of our Progressive acquaintance with the ways of God as well as of our becoming more and more God-like

7. When therefore we speak about growing in grace or moving from glory to glory, we are at the same time talking about growing in love and spiritual maturity and moving toward perfection, which is the human pursuit of the perfection of God

---

PAUSE FOR REVIEW

SEE QUESTIONS BELOW TO HELP GUIDE YOUR DISCUSSIONS. YOU MAY ADD YOUR OWN QUESTIONS THAT MAY HAVE COME OUT OF YOUR STUDY EXPERIENCE TOGETHER

EVALUATION/DISCUSSION QUESTIONS

1. **What are some other terms that may be used to describe human glory?**

2. **What is the difference between the glory of God and human glory?**

3. **List and discuss three characteristics of the glory of God**

4. **We believe that we shall see God in all of His glory in eternity. Share with us some ways that you believe that the glory of God is being manifested now**

5. **Do you believe that as Christians we are moving from glory to glory? Share with us how you think this is happening**

Moving From Glory to Glory
(Section Two)

1. Perfection, the goal of spiritual transformation is therefore the result of total surrender to the perfect will and purpose of God

2. By virtue of our redemption, Christ has effectively reintroduced us to the life and glory of God

3. Our becoming Christ-like or more like God should not be taken however, to mean that we are seeking to acquire deity or to become divine

4. Remember now that we are not necessarily sharing the glory of God as much as we are being drawn into His glorious and eternal presence

5. According to 2 Corinthians 5:4, the One who has prepared us for this very thing—eternity, and our living in His glory— is God

6. Moving from glory to glory is about the completion of our spiritual transformation

7. Our moving from glory to glory should therefore be taken to mean that we are caught up in a process whereby we are learning more of the ways of God and learning more of His love and will

8. Our moving from glory to glory is also our moving toward perfection

9. In this life, the more we behold the presence and power of God in our lives, and as we surrender to that power working in us, the more we are elevated to become like Him

—

| PAUSE FOR REVIEW |
SEE QUESTIONS BELOW TO HELP GUIDE YOUR DISCUSSIONS. YOU MAY ADD YOUR OWN QUESTIONS THAT MAY HAVE COME OUT OF YOUR STUDY EXPERIENCE TOGETHER

EVALUATION/DISCUSSION QUESTIONS

1. **Jesus says we should be perfect even as our heavenly Father is perfect.**

2. **What do you think Christian perfection is?**

3. **What do you understand when the writer speaks of the "divine saturation of us?"**

4. **What do you think the writer means when he says in Philippians 3:20-21 that our citizenship is in heaven?**

CHAPTER THREE

CHRISTIAN WORSHIP

Devotional Exercise
>Welcome/Greetings
>Sharing of prayer concerns
>Prayer
>Hymn(s) of the day
>Scripture selection(s) for today

Prayer:

Dear Lord, thank You for coming where we are. We are moved by Your desire to have fellowship and communion with us. We give You honor, glory, and praise because You are worthy. We thank You for inviting us to worship and for stirring up our faithful response to You. All that we know You have taught us through the gift of Your Son Jesus Christ. Continue, we pray, to enlighten our minds. By the inspiration of You Holy Spirit, empower us to live and worship You because we know that You are our Creator, Redeemer through Christ Jesus our Lord, and Sanctifier through the power and authority of the Holy Spirit. Teach us we pray, to differentiate between sincerity and pretense in worship, and move us by the Holy Spirit to worship You so that what we do and say will be in Spirit and in truth and for your glory. This we pray in the name of Jesus, Amen!

Suggested Scripture Readings:
>2 Kn 17:36; 1 Chr 16:29; Ps 29:2; 99:5; Mt 4:10; Jn 4:24; Rev 14:7

Hymns:
>"Open The Eyes Of My Heart Lord"
>"Be Thou My Vision"
>"Holy, Holy, Holy…"
>"O Worship The King"
>"To God Be The Glory"
>"Joyful, Joyful, We Adore Thee"
>"O For A Thousand Tongues To Sing"
>"We Have A Story To Tell To The Nations"

Objectives:
To help us:

- Develop an understanding of what worship is
- Develop appreciation of the nature purpose of worship
- See how worship is properly a divine initiative and human response
- See how knowledge of God relates to proper worship of God
- Develop appreciation of worship as communion and participation
- Develop an appreciation of worship as a continuous and doxological process
- See worship as essentially relational and participative
- Understand worship as continuous communion
- Develop an understanding of the channel of mediation in worship
- Understand our motives for worship

1. OVERVIEW

This chapter is an examination of the correlation between proper knowledge of God and proper worship of God. Proper knowledge and worship of God have to do with knowing and worshipping God as He exists in unity with, and as He manifests Himself through Jesus the Son, in the presence and power of the Holy Spirit. The God whom we worship is, and should always be understood as Creator, Redeemer, and Sanctifier. Knowing God the Father as Creator, who reveals Himself through Christ the Son as Redeemer, and through the Holy Spirit as Sanctifier, is critical for our understanding of the dialogue that takes place between God and us in worship as well as in our life experiences.

True worship begins with recognizing and responding to God as He exists and is manifested through the Son, in the power of the Holy Spirit. Worship that is true is worship that is in response to God as He exists, not as we desire Him to be. Otherwise, we would be worshipping a god after our own making and design rather than the God who made us after His own likeness.

Worship, indeed, the Christian life, is a process of transformation that begins with an engaged understanding of the unity of the Father, Son, and Holy Spirit. An engaged understanding of the unity of the Father, Son, and Holy Spirit is necessary because understanding how the Father, Son and Holy Spirit work in our lives and worship will lead us to embrace the fullness of God who is intent on having a relationship with us. Our worship of God is both a communion and a participation in the already perfect worship and service of the Jesus the Son to God the Father. In worship, the Holy Spirit facilitates and empowers our worship, while Jesus the Son, is our Mediator and High Priest and therefore the medium of our worship dialogue with God. This ongoing dialogue in worship and our motives for worship will form constituent parts of this portion of our conversation.

PAUSE FOR LESSON REVIEW
QUESTIONS/COMMENTS/CLARIFICATIONS
BREAK INTO GROUP DISCUSSIONS

2. WHAT IS WORSHIP?

1. Worship is a divine initiative

2. Since worship is a divine initiative and a human response to a divine invitation, worship is communion with God

3. While we gather in buildings and locations to worship, worship really takes place in the human heart and mind where nothing else matters but God

4. Worship is all that the body of Christ does in faithful response to God's invitation and gift of participation with the distinct purpose of giving glory to God

5. Worship therefore becomes an enriched spiritual experience with God and an occasion to witness to others about His mighty power, grace and love

—

PAUSE FOR LESSON REVIEW
QUESTIONS/COMMENTS/CLARIFICATIONS
BREAK INTO GROUP DISCUSSIONS

EVALUATION/DISCUSSION QUESTIONS

1. **What is worship and how do we encounter God in worship?**

2. **Why do you think the human heart is so important to God in worship?**

3. **"Worship is a place." What do you think this means and how would you describe that place?**

4. **Based on your experience of worship, please share with us your understanding of worship as a gift of participation**

5. **Discuss with each other how worship may be an enriched spiritual experience**

3. KNOWLEDGE OF GOD AND TRUE WORSHIP

1. Our journey with God begins with our recognition and knowledge of who He is – GOD!

2. While our faith journey begins with an awareness of God and spills over onto worshipful adoration of God, and while the Christian life begins in and through the activity of God who calls us together and meets us in worship, worship is not the only place where God meets us

3. In crisis, tragedy, or when driven by despair, we may go to God for ourselves; but in worship we go to God for God

4. Since it is in the context of our historical and empirical existence that we come face to face with the Object of our faith, we need to begin with worship as a place where we are summoned to respond to God

5. Our knowledge and subsequent worship of God is the beginning of a remarkable journey with God that leads to our progressive transformation and subsequent eternity with Him

6. Knowledge of God leads to informed and proper worship of God

7. Understanding the worship process may therefore lead to real, living, and participative experience through Christ who taught us, and the Holy Spirit who stirs us to respond to God's invitation to worship

8. Valid and sincere worship is the kind of worship that reaches to the Father, through the Son, in the power of the Holy Spirit

9. While perfect knowledge is not required to worship God, our desire to worship should always be driven by what we have come to know about God

10. Without knowledge, we cannot participate in the divine life

---

PAUSE FOR REVIEW

SEE QUESTIONS BELOW TO HELP GUIDE YOUR DISCUSSIONS. YOU MAY ADD YOUR OWN QUESTIONS THAT MAY HAVE COME OUT OF YOUR STUDY EXPERIENCE TOGETHER

EVALUATION/DISCUSSION QUESTIONS

1. **How important do you think knowledge of God is for worship and life?**

2. **To what extent do you think knowledge of God and worship may change your attitude towards worship?**

3. **What motivates you to worship God?**

4. **In what ways do you think knowledge and understanding of worship may lead to more intentional participation?**

5. **What is your understanding of the channel of worship?**

4. WORSHIP:
A DIVINE INITIATIVE AND A HUMAN RESPONSE
(SECTION ONE)

1. The tendency to think that worship is something that we worshippers initiate and therefore "do" is a common misconception that leads to common and often routine worship

2. Because we think that worship is something that we initiate, we go into worship trying to invoke and call forth the presence of God through our so-called prayers of invocation

3. Worship is an event in which God comes to us and draws us to Himself through Christ in the power of the Holy Spirit

4. As the Holy Spirit enables us to recognize the nearness and initiative of God, He also helps us to respond faithfully to that nearness with worship

5. As a divine initiative, it is God, by the inspiration of the Holy Spirit that stirs within our hearts the desire for communion and fellowship

6. The misconception of worship as something that we do and initiate is one that has carried over into the act of worship itself and needs to be corrected

—

PAUSE FOR REVIEW

SEE QUESTIONS BELOW TO HELP GUIDE YOUR DISCUSSIONS. YOU MAY
ADD YOUR OWN QUESTIONS THAT MAY HAVE COME OUT OF YOUR STUDY
EXPERIENCE TOGETHER

EVALUATION/DISCUSSION QUESTIONS

1. **"Worship is not about us." What do you gather from this statement?**

2. **Worship is not something that we do. Explain**

3. **What do you understand by worship as a divine initiative?**

WORSHIP: A DIVINE INITIATIVE AND A HUMAN RESPONSE (SECTION TWO)

1. Worship is likely to become idolatrous when it is no longer our response to God and His divine initiative, but a projection of our learnedness, our theatrics, our know-how, our personal achievements, our own self-centered aspirations, and our human abilities aimed at satisfying our own emotions and entertaining the masses

2. If we think that worship is something that we do, we are, above all persons, most bankrupt because we are also saying that the only priesthood is our priesthood, the only offering is our offering, and the only intercession is our intercession[8]

3. Worship, it must be stressed, is not a spectator event or something that we leisurely and mindlessly observe

4. Our response in worship is what Thompson calls "a response to a response"[9]

---

[8] Torrance, _Worship and Community,_ 1996

[9] Thompson, 100

5. In worship, then, our participation and response are gifts of the Holy Spirit

6. By extension, our response to God's initiative with our kneeling at the altar, and our communion at the Lord's Table are gifts of the Holy Spirit

7. If worship is to be more than appearance, exacted homage, and a cluster of routine theatrical procedures, we need to urgently recognize that it is God who lovingly makes the first move in drawing us to Himself

8. When in worship, we allow Jesus by His example and knowledge of the Father[10] to inspire our worship of God, worship is likely to become more meaningful for us

9. While worship requires our response and participation, and while the things we bring to worship are important contributions to the worship experience, we need to leave room for God to surprise us

10. The things that we bring to the worship encounter, such as our fine buildings, fine- tuned instruments, human expediencies, and oratory skills, are all together good

11. The Holy Spirit who invokes within us the need and the desire to respond to God's initiative, and moves us to rely on the sole priesthood of Christ, also gives life/vigor and meaning to our worship of God

———

---

[10] Jn 15:15

PAUSE FOR REVIEW

SEE QUESTIONS BELOW TO HELP GUIDE YOUR DISCUSSIONS. YOU MAY
ADD YOUR OWN QUESTIONS THAT MAY HAVE COME OUT OF YOUR STUDY
EXPERIENCE TOGETHER

EVALUATION/DISCUSSION QUESTIONS

1. Why do you think it is important to leave room for God to surprise us in worship?

2. How can we leave room for God to surprise us?

3. What are some of the contributions that we bring to worship?

4. What would you consider the most important contribution that we can bring to worship?

5. Where do life and vigor/passion in worship come from?

5. CHRISTIAN WORSHIP AS COMMUNION AND PARTICIPATION (SECTION ONE)

1. The Bible is filled with references to the communal and participative nature of worship

2. Worship, as communion, our sharing in the Word and Sacraments, and in the life and ministry of Christ, is most appropriately celebrated in the spirit and context of the Christian community

3. In what, then, are we participating?

—

PAUSE FOR REVIEW
SEE QUESTIONS BELOW TO HELP GUIDE YOUR DISCUSSIONS. YOU MAY ADD YOUR OWN QUESTIONS THAT MAY HAVE COME OUT OF YOUR STUDY EXPERIENCE TOGETHER

EVALUATION/DISCUSSION QUESTIONS

1. **How has this lesson helped your understanding of worship?**

2. **Why do you think it is important to know God in order to ascribe true worship to Him?**

3. **What does it mean to participate in worship and not just observe worship?**

CHRISTIAN WORSHIP AS COMMUNION AND PARTICIPATION (SECTION TWO)

1. If worship is communion and participation, the communion and the fellowship that we share with God and each other in worship need to spill over into the Christian community

2. Christian worship and fellowship are not only Sunday morning events

3. Worship should never be compartmentalized nor should it be an occasional experience

4. As a Christian and a pastor, I have painfully observed the absence of sustained fellowship in the Christian community

5. Perhaps if we were to acknowledge that we will spend eternity in heaven with each other and with Christ, we would begin to develop the good sense of fellowshipping together so that we can begin to have "a little heaven down here"

6. When we understand worship as relational, participative, and an overflow of our fellowship and communion with God and with each other, we may become more serious about being in alignment with each other as well as being in alignment with the will of God

7. The point to remember is that worship is central to our lives

—

PAUSE FOR REVIEW

SEE QUESTIONS BELOW TO HELP GUIDE YOUR DISCUSSIONS. YOU MAY ADD YOUR OWN QUESTIONS THAT MAY HAVE COME OUT OF YOUR STUDY EXPERIENCE TOGETHER

EVALUATION/DISCUSSION QUESTIONS

1. **What do participation and communion mean to you as they relate to worship and community living?**

2. **Are you encouraged by this information to participate more in the process of worship and the life of the church? If so, please tell us how**

3. **What do you suggest that we do to enhance worship in our church?**

4. **Giving examples, please say how you have benefited from today's lesson**

5. **Using the following suggested pointers, discuss why you think the Christian community today may not have a deep sense of relationship?**

   a. **We do not have time**
   b. **We do not take the time to know each other**

  c. **We do not care enough to know each other's needs**
  d. **Our cultures are so different**
  e. **Other reasons (excuses)**

6. Worship As A Dialogue: The Channel Of Mediation

1. Because worship is communion and participation, it becomes essentially a dialogue between God and human beings

2. This dialogue begins and ends with God

3. Grasping this essential principle of the channel of mediation in worship is necessary for our understanding of God's flow of grace to us in worship and life

4. True worship, true prayers, and true praise are emphatically God-centered and channeled through Christ in the power of the Holy Spirit

5. Because of the mediatory role of Jesus and the sanctifying and sustaining power of the Holy Spirit, the place where God meets us is not merely in the external forms of worship, but in places of the heart, mind, and soul

—

EVALUATION/DISCUSSION QUESTIONS

1. How does an understanding of worship as relational and participative help to raise your commitment to worship?

2. How does an understanding of worship, as a continuous process, help you to order your life around God at all times?

3. Was today's lesson helpful for your understanding of the channel or medium of communication in worship?

4. How has this understanding of worship as a dialogue impacted your attitude toward prayer, praise, and worship?

5. Based on today's lesson, do you see yourself as having a clearer understanding of worship? Please say how.

7. MOTIVES FOR WORSHIP (SECTION ONE)

1. We are motivated to worship God first of all because we recognize who God is and because God invites us to

2. We are moved to worship God because we experience God taking hold of us as the First Cause and at the core of our existence

3. We worship God because we are moved by the Holy Spirit to celebrate God

4. Love motivates us to worship God

5. We worship and celebrate God with joyful shouts of praise because we are aware of His involvement in getting us through some of life's greatest challenges

6. In life and in worship, praise does three, though not exclusive, things

—

PAUSE FOR LESSON REVIEW
QUESTIONS/COMMENTS/CLARIFICATIONS
BREAK INTO GROUP DISCUSSIONS

EVALUATION/DISCUSSION QUESTIONS

1. **List three reasons why we worship God?**

2. **Have you ever felt like not worshipping? If yes, why? If no, why not?**

3. **How do you benefit from worship?**

4. **Why do you think God is seeking fellowship and communion with us?**

5. **What role do you think love plays in our worship of God?**

6. **What does it mean for you to celebrate God in worship?**

7. List three things for which you are motivated to give God praise

MOTIVES FOR WORSHIP
(SECTION TWO)

1. I want to make it abundantly clear that while a shout of praise is usually a spontaneous expression of joy and praise for an extraordinary blessing of God, no one should be compelled to shout or made to feel that they are ungodly if they do not shout

2. We should never belittle or disparage those who elect not to verbalize or articulate their praise

3. For those who may want to insist on having quiet times during worship, they should not, however, get mad when "Sister So and So" and "Brother So and So" get really joyful and glad in the Lord

4. Some of us just love to praise God

5. As the old spiritual says: "There ain't no harm to praise the Lord"

6. We are motivated to worship God because He is our strength

7. Some of us may not always have the energy to move all week because of sickness in our bodies

8. We are motivated to worship God because we also recognize that in Him, our value is elevated and our person-hood is liberated

9. Let us consider for a moment how worship changes and affirms our human value

—

| PAUSE FOR REVIEW |
SEE QUESTIONS BELOW TO HELP GUIDE YOUR DISCUSSIONS. YOU MAY
ADD YOUR OWN QUESTIONS THAT MAY HAVE COME OUT OF YOUR STUDY
EXPERIENCE TOGETHER

EVALUATION/DISCUSSION QUESTIONS

1. **What motivates you to worship God?**

2. **Have you experienced God this week/recently? (List three ways that you have experienced God that have moved you to worship)**

3. **How has this lesson on motives for worship helped your understanding of worship as a place for thanksgiving and praise?**

4. **How does an understanding of worship encourage you to participate or become more engaged in the process of worship and the life of the church?**

MOTIVES FOR WORSHIP (SECTION THREE)

1. The experience of God's presence and help in our lives all through the week motivates us to assemble together so that we may jubilantly gather up our joys and our concerns in a bundle of praise as we testify to others about our experience with God

2. We come together to worship God because in His presence we have assurance and acceptance

3. When worship is a part of our lives and our hearts are in tuned to God, we feel secure in the presence of God

4. Based on who we know God to be, and the benefits that He bestows upon us when we lavishly praise His holy name, many of us are enthusiastic about worship and do not necessarily wait for Sunday morning to "have church"

5. We are motivated to worship because God matters

6. Here is a joyful report!

7. We are motivated to worship God because we recognize that through Jesus Christ, the grace of God comes to us with hope and the promise of eternity

8. We are motivated to worship and glorify God because we recognize that in life, worship, and witness, the Holy Spirit takes us, broken earthen vessels, and replenishes and transforms us into the heavenly treasures of God's holiness[11]

9. Consequently, the cross should not be viewed as a sacrifice that seeks to satisfy the anger of an offended God

10. John Layton seconded that motion when he penned these words of praise:

    "We'll praise the Lord for He is great,
    And in His presence angels wait;
    All heaven is swelling with His praise,
    Shall we not, too, our anthems raise…? (From the Hymn *"We'll Praise The Lord"*)

---

[11] 2 Cor 4:7

PAUSE FOR REVIEW

SEE QUESTIONS BELOW TO HELP GUIDE YOUR DISCUSSIONS. YOU MAY ADD YOUR OWN QUESTIONS THAT MAY HAVE COME OUT OF YOUR STUDY EXPERIENCE TOGETHER

EVALUATION/DISCUSSION QUESTIONS

1. What motivates you to worship God?

2. Have you experienced God this week/recently? (List three ways that you have experienced God that have moved you to worship)

3. How has this lesson on our motives for worship helped your understanding of worship as a place for thanksgiving and praise?

4. How does an understanding of worship encourage you to participate or become more engaged in the process of worship and the life of the church?

5. How do you think an understanding of today's lesson can lead to revitalized worship?

6. How have you benefited from today's lesson?

If true worship comes from our understanding or knowledge of God, then it is essential to have knowledge and understanding of the liturgy that directs our attention to the only true God who is worthy of our worship and praise. This is a good point from which to launch our conversation concerning some selected components of the liturgy of worship. Here we shall also examine the purposes of the liturgy, and the implications of living liturgical and doxological lives.

Chapter Four

The Liturgy Of Worship

Devotional Exercise
    Welcome/Greetings
    Sharing of prayer concerns
    Prayer
    Hymn(s) of the day
    Scripture selection(s) for today

Prayer:
    Enter my heart anew today, oh Lord. Fill my heart with desires for You. Fill my thoughts with contemplations of Your merciful ways. Fill my mind with Your Word. Touch my tongue dear God, so that my mouth shall shout aloud what my mind is already aware of and what my heart desires to raise, Your eternal praise. Guide me in every area of my life so that I may bring glory to Your holy name by all that I do to serve You. This I pray in the precious name of Jesus, Amen!

Suggested Scripture Readings: Ps. 150; Mt. 5:16; Rom. 12: 18, 15: 17-19, 27; Gal. 5:25; 1 Pet. 1:12-19

Hymns:
    "O Worship the King"
    "Worship His Majesty"
    "Open The Eyes Of My Heart Lord"
    "One God, One Faith, One Baptism"
    "O Come, O Come Emmanuel"
    "It Is Well With My Soul"
    "Fill My Cup Lord"
    "I Know It Was The Blood"

Objectives:
To help us:

- Develop an understanding of and appreciation for selected components of worship
- Develop an understanding of the place and purpose of the liturgy

- See and appreciate the liturgical components of worship as icons that direct us to God
- Understand the channel of communication in worship

1. Overview

Since it is in worship that many practicing Christians are made aware of liturgical forms and practices, without being exhaustive, selected liturgical forms and practices will be discussed. The goal is to foster understanding of the theological and doctrinal imports of the liturgy in worship. I also set out to show how practicing worshippers might be aided by the liturgy in their understanding of God. Certainly, when the content and purpose of the liturgy are understood, the potential for worshippers discovering meaning and reaching greater levels of intentional participation becomes a more realistic goal. Such understanding may also have spiritually transforming benefits. When we understand the purpose and design of the liturgy, the potential for meaningful and intentional worship may also become attainable. Since understanding of a process often leads to sense-making, and even a greater degree of participation in that process, understanding the liturgy and its purpose in worship has fascinating possibilities and may lead to worshippers' renewed awareness of God to whom the liturgy ultimately points.

Discussions of liturgical components will be limited to the call to worship, preaching, Baptism, Holy Communion, and the doxology. In our discussion on the call to worship, we shall see that long before the pastor or worship leader calls us to worship, God has already done so. The invitation and call to worship is God's. We are simply carriers, distributors, and faithful respondents to it. As pastors and worship leaders, our task, at best, becomes a reminder for worshippers to respond to the call of God who comes near and draws us through the Holy Spirit to worship Him. The call to worship is a point at which the Holy Spirit rather than the pastor or worship leader calls forth a scattered people to lift high their united praise of God in the true Spirit of worship.

Discussion on preaching, as a word from the Lord, is intended to show how preaching is a change agent. As such, we shall see that preaching is both a source of information as well as a channel of inspiration and change. As a source of information, preaching encourages change by informing the mind and stirring up the human intellect. As inspiration, preaching speaks to the human heart in order to invoke the right attitude for living out that change.

Regarding Baptism and Holy Communion, it is my intention to show how, through the sacraments of Baptism and Holy Communion, God is intent on giving us new starts, and having sustained fellowship and communion with us. The goal is also to demonstrate how relentless God is about drawing us into communion with Him. How God the Father works in unity with the Son and the Holy Spirit to achieve that goal will constitute critical components of our discussion and subsequent understanding.

In our exploration of the doxology, I seek to show that the doxology is not limited to the worship ingathering and the context of formal worship. The doxology also extends beyond the formal liturgy to encompass the way we live our lives as witnesses to the power and grace of God. I will argue then, that the doxology and the benediction should rightly be considered precursors for continuous Christian living, mission, and service to God in the world, rather than being thought of as liturgical proclamations that worship has ended.

Based on an informative and practical paradigm, our discussion of the liturgy is intended to promote the development of a synthesis of worship, liturgical practices, pastoral leadership, and worshippers' response. The objective is to encourage mutual elevation of laity participation and pastoral leadership through the recognition of, and a working toward, a common consensus on the purpose of liturgical practices.

—

PAUSE FOR QUESTIONS/COMMENTS/CLARIFICATIONS

2. THE PURPOSE OF THE LITURGY

1. What is liturgy and what is its purpose?

2. The liturgy is a coming together of selected forms, words, and actions that are designed to open the worshipper's awareness of God and the selected sequences of that particular worship service

3. As we have already established, God initiates worship

4. Within the context of the Sunday morning worship service, the liturgy is a sort of disclosure of pastoral intent that seeks to deepen the worshipper's receptivity and openness to God

5. The Holy Spirit is therefore the inspiration and director of the liturgy

6. The structure of the liturgy should be such that it not only makes us aware of who God is and His presence among us; it should also encourage us to become caught up in the outpouring life and activity of God in worship

---

PAUSE FOR REVIEW

SEE QUESTIONS BELOW TO HELP GUIDE YOUR DISCUSSIONS. YOU MAY ADD YOUR OWN QUESTIONS THAT MAY HAVE COME OUT OF YOUR STUDY EXPERIENCE TOGETHER

EVALUATION/DISCUSSION QUESTIONS

1. **In your own words, what is the liturgy?**

2. **What do you see as some of the benefits of having a liturgy of worship?**

3. **What is meant by the term "God is our primary Liturgist?"**

3. SELECTED COMPONENTS OF WORSHIP

A. The Call To Worship: A Reminder and Preparation for Worship

1. The call to worship is a component of the liturgy that may be used to draw our attention to the event of worship

2. When then, does the worship service really begin?

3. Because worship requires preparation, the entire family should be engaged in the preparation process

4. A period of preparation, a day or two before our actual day of worship, may also serve to develop as well as nurture our faithfulness, passionate anticipation and desire for worship

5. The call to worship, then, is the point at which the Holy Spirit, through the pastor or worship leader, calls forth God's people for intentional and passionate worship

6. We are called for inward gathering for three reasons

———

EVALUATION/DISCUSSION QUESTIONS

1. What are some examples of religious materials that can be used as call to worship in a formal worship service?

2. Worship requires preparation. What are some things that you and your family do in advance to prepare for worship?

3. From a spiritual point of view, share with us who is largely responsible for calling God's gathered people to worship?

B. Preaching
(Section One)

1. Preaching is an integral part of the liturgy of worship

2. The primary task of preaching is to change the human heart by drawing people's attention to the Good News of God's redeeming love, mercy and grace through the Lord Jesus. By extension, preaching has five major roles

3. The first role of preaching is to invoke awareness

4. The second role of preaching is to be a change agent in the process of interpreting and encouraging faith

5. The third role of preaching is to re-present Christ

6. The fourth role of preaching is to hold us accountable to God and to each other

7. The fifth role of preaching is to encourage discipleship

8. The sixth role of preaching is to offer hope

PAUSE FOR REVIEW

SEE QUESTIONS BELOW TO HELP GUIDE YOUR DISCUSSIONS. YOU MAY ADD YOUR OWN QUESTIONS THAT MAY HAVE COME OUT OF YOUR STUDY EXPERIENCE TOGETHER

EVALUATION/DISCUSSION QUESTIONS

1. **How would you define preaching?**

2. **Why do you think preaching is an important part of the liturgy of worship?**

3. **The primary task of preaching is to draw people's attention to the Good News of God's redeeming love**

4. **Please take a moment to list and discuss the six steps by which preaching accomplishes its purpose**

5. **Why do you think people respond differently to preaching?**

6. **Why do you think that merely hearing the preached word is not enough?**

7. **Using examples, share with us how you think preaching encourages discipleship**

8. **Please share with us your personal response and appreciation for preaching. Be sure to include how preaching has personally impacted your life.**

Preaching
(Section Two)

1. While some may have chosen to preach, others are called and anointed by God to do so[12]

2. For preaching to have the desired impact of bringing about awareness and change in the human life and condition, the preacher and those who hear the word, cannot settle for faulty theology

3. Before the word is preached, if it is to have the desired effects, it must first be God's Word and revelation imparted to the preacher by the Holy Spirit

4. Our receptiveness to preaching is often an indication of our own understanding and encounters with God

5. As scriptures attest, many people can listen to the same message but leave with totally different takes or interpretations of it

6. Preaching in and by itself cannot change us

7. Merely hearing the word is never enough

---

[12] Mt 20:16

8. Preaching is both a challenge and a source of comfort for the preacher as well as for those who hear and respond with faith to the preached word

—

| PAUSE FOR REVIEW |

SEE QUESTIONS BELOW TO HELP GUIDE YOUR DISCUSSIONS. YOU MAY ADD YOUR OWN QUESTIONS THAT MAY HAVE COME OUT OF YOUR STUDY EXPERIENCE TOGETHER

EVALUATION/DISCUSSION QUESTIONS

1. **What do you think is the major difference between a preacher called to preach and one who chooses to perhaps as a career choice or because he/she has oratory skills?**

2. **What is faulty theology?**

3. **Please take a moment to share with us how your experience of God and understanding of scripture help you to better understand a preached message**

4. **According to the writer, "Preaching in and by itself cannot save us." How would you explain that statement?**

5. **Discuss amongst yourselves the point that "Preaching is both a challenge and a source of comfort."**

C. The Sacrament of Holy Baptism

(i) Overview

Baptism and Holy Communion are the two Sacraments practiced by most Protestant churches. A Sacrament is a special act of worship that was instituted by Jesus. Sacraments are means of grace. They are means of grace because they are ritualistic forms and practices that direct our attention to God's gracious acts of redemption, mercy, love, and life transforming presence in our lives as well as in the world. Sacraments are means by which God's love and grace are imparted to us. God's love conveyed to us through Jesus Christ is intended to transform us. We do not believe that the sacraments have some sort of magical powers to do so. What we do believe is that the sacraments of Baptism and Holy Communion are channels through which God makes grace available to those, who by faith, receive them and accept His Christ as their Savior and Lord.

Participation in these Sacraments does not automatically make us holy. Participation in these Sacraments helps to stir up our awareness and makes us receptive to the availability of God's divine grace and love. Our response of faith to God's love makes us receptive to the holiness and righteousness of God from whom alone righteousness comes. Our righteousness is attributed to us by faith through grace. Baptism therefore initiates us into a grace-filled relationship with God. Holy Communion keeps us in faithful fellowship as the Holy Spirit works in us to remind us of the sacrifice of Christ on the cross as well as to draw us into habitual, yet faithful communion with the Father and the Son and with each other.

—

PAUSE FOR LESSON REVIEW
QUESTIONS/COMMENTS/CLARIFICATIONS
BREAK INTO GROUP DISCUSSIONS

(ii) What is Baptism?
(Section One)

1. Baptism is a Christian Sacrament involving a ritual application or use of water

2. Baptism, before it is ours, is first the Baptism of Christ

3. Baptism is a sign or public indicator of our submission to Christ, as well as a sign of who we have become in Christ

4. In conjunction with water Baptism, we are also baptized in the Holy Spirit

5. Baptism is the beginning of the believer's union with Christ

6. Regeneration or rebirth is not our work; it is a gift

—

PAUSE FOR REVIEW

SEE QUESTIONS BELOW TO HELP GUIDE YOUR DISCUSSIONS. YOU MAY ADD YOUR OWN QUESTIONS THAT MAY HAVE COME OUT OF YOUR STUDY EXPERIENCE TOGETHER

EVALUATION/DISCUSSION QUESTIONS

1. **Please take a moment to discuss the different forms that Baptism can take**
2. **What do you understand when the writer says "Baptism before it is ours, is first the Baptism of Christ?"**
3. **What is your understanding of the Baptism of the Holy Spirit?**
4. **In what ways is Baptism considered a new birth?**
5. **How is Baptism or rebirth a gift? Please give examples where you can**

What Is Baptism?
(Section Two)

1. How then, does rebirth or regeneration take place? And which comes first, faith or regeneration?
2. Let us now address the question of "How does rebirth or regeneration take place?" First…
3. Second, upon hearing the preached word, the Holy Spirit stirs us from within so that our cognition would invoke our thoughts; our thoughts would then lead to the contemplation of righteousness

4. Third, because of our awareness of God and His holiness, we are moved to bow in humility and confess our sins and shortcomings before Him

5. Fourth, regeneration comes when our attention is redirected to Christ and His atoning sacrifice on the Cross at Calvary

6. Again, rebirth or regeneration is not our work, it is God's work

7. This matter of divine initiative or God's holy influence is important for our understanding of divine grace in the process of our salvation

8. Regeneration or rebirth is therefore God's gracious and benevolent fixing of us[13]

9. You may be asking, "What then does the Apostle Paul mean when he said in Philippians 2:12, 'work out your own salvation with fear and trembling?'"

10. Because it is God who wills to save us and because it is God who shows mercy, we deserve none of the credit for our redemption

11. When we are baptized, we are baptized into Christ

——

---

[13] Tit 3:5-7; Jas 1:16-18

PAUSE FOR REVIEW

SEE QUESTIONS BELOW TO HELP GUIDE YOUR DISCUSSIONS. YOU MAY
ADD YOUR OWN QUESTIONS THAT MAY HAVE COME OUT OF YOUR STUDY
EXPERIENCE TOGETHER

EVALUATION/DISCUSSION QUESTIONS

1. **Which comes first, regeneration or faith?**

2. **Please share with us your understanding of the process or stages of regeneration**

3. **What do you think the author means when he says, "Regeneration or rebirth is therefore God's benevolent fixing of us?" What scripture would you use to support that affirmation?**

(iii) Baptism and the Death and Resurrection of Jesus

1. Baptism is often viewed as an imitation of the death and resurrection of Jesus

2. Through Baptism, the believer is united with Christ in His death and is raised to a new life of faith in His resurrection

3. At our Baptism, emphasis is not so much on the act, but on the result

—

PAUSE FOR REVIEW

SEE QUESTIONS BELOW TO HELP GUIDE YOUR DISCUSSIONS. YOU MAY
ADD YOUR OWN QUESTIONS THAT MAY HAVE COME OUT OF YOUR STUDY
EXPERIENCE TOGETHER

EVALUATION/DISCUSSION QUESTIONS

1. **Why do you think that Baptism is often compared to the death and resurrection of Jesus?**

2. **Using scriptures, share with each other how more emphasis is placed on the result rather than the act of Baptism itself**

3. **What thoughts or reminders has this lesson brought up for you as you remember your Baptism?**

(iv) The Baptism of Children
(Section One)

1. Should children be baptized?

2. As a believer and practitioner in the liturgical faith practices of the church, I do not feel obligated to justify the Baptism of children to anyone

3. Here are some questions to consider as we contemplate the matter:
    a. Are children not part of God's kingdom?
    b. Were children also not made by God to share in God's eternity?
    c. Do children not have the right and access to the kingdom of heaven?
    d. Did Christ not die so that children too may live?
    e. If we say that the Baptism of Christ was our Baptism, was Christ not also baptized for children?

4. Let us highlight for a moment a few Scriptures that speak to the baptisms of households

5. While children may not be able to make independent choices for Baptism, it is not our adult responsibility to deny them Baptism

—

PAUSE FOR REVIEW

SEE QUESTIONS BELOW TO HELP GUIDE YOUR DISCUSSIONS. YOU MAY ADD YOUR OWN QUESTIONS THAT MAY HAVE COME OUT OF YOUR STUDY EXPERIENCE TOGETHER

EVALUATION/DISCUSSION QUESTIONS

1. **What is your understanding of the Bible regarding the Baptism of children?**

2. **If Baptism is a sort of initiation into the household of faith and therefore the kingdom of heaven, do you believe that heaven or eternity is reserved only for adults?**

3. **What does the Bible say about the Baptism of households?**

The Baptism of Children
(Section Two)

1. Some people base their objection to children's Baptism on the grounds that children have not developed the cognitive ability to understand the spiritual significance and faith principles of Baptism

2. Baptism is a gift of grace that is not made effectual by human understanding but by the human faith response to the grace of God offered to us through Christ

3. Mental capacity and cognitive development are not prerequisites for salvation

4. If we were to look back at circumcision in the Old Testament for example, we will see that the male child did not make the decision to be circumcised

—

PAUSE FOR REVIEW
SEE QUESTIONS BELOW TO HELP GUIDE YOUR DISCUSSIONS. YOU MAY
ADD YOUR OWN QUESTIONS THAT MAY HAVE COME OUT OF YOUR STUDY
EXPERIENCE TOGETHER

EVALUATION/DISCUSSION QUESTIONS

1. **Share with each other some of the arguments used in objection to the baptism of children**

2. **Do you think that mental capacity or the cognitive ability to understand the spiritual implications of Baptism is a precondition for salvation?**

3. **How would you respond to the claim that children are not old enough to make the decision for Baptism in light of the circumcision of children in the Old Testament?**

(v) Baptism: A Replacement for Circumcision?

1. What is circumcision and what is the religious importance of the practice?

2. With the exception of ritual washing for purification, there are no parallels to Christian Baptism in the Old Testament.

3. John's Baptism, picked up by the Early Church, influenced no doubt by Jesus' acceptance of it, took on new spiritual significance including Baptism as union with Christ and the Baptism of the Holy Spirit

4. Baptism in the New Testament is a reflection of the same emphasis on covenant relationship as was circumcision in the Old Testament with one fundamental difference

5. Actually, even in the Old Testament, true righteousness was never found in circumcision but in walking obediently with God

---

PAUSE FOR REVIEW

SEE QUESTIONS BELOW TO HELP GUIDE YOUR DISCUSSIONS. YOU MAY ADD YOUR OWN QUESTIONS THAT MAY HAVE COME OUT OF YOUR STUDY EXPERIENCE TOGETHER

EVALUATION/DISCUSSION QUESTIONS

1. **What do you see as the most outstanding (spiritual) difference between circumcision and Baptism as practiced in the Old and New Testaments?**

2. **Using the practices of circumcision and Baptism as the basis for your discussion, share with us what you think is the basis of true righteousness?**

3. **What do you think are some of the common emphases that both Baptism and circumcision share?**

(vi) The Holy Spirit and The Effects of Baptism
(Section One)

1. To be baptized is to receive the Holy Spirit because Baptism marks the Spirit's entry into the Christian's life[14]

2. Though we are baptized once, we are never left alone

---

[14] Acts 2:38

3. Through Baptism, the Holy Spirit is the believer's point of contact and entry into intimacy with God

4. As a work of the Holy Spirit, Baptism signifies forgiveness

5. It is the Holy Spirit that draws our attention to Christ, urges us on to repentance by convicting us of sin, and making us aware of the value of righteousness[15]

6. Through Baptism, Christ who dwells within us, permeates our hearts, minds and souls, and unites our entire being with the life of God

—

PAUSE FOR REVIEW

SEE QUESTIONS BELOW TO HELP GUIDE YOUR DISCUSSIONS. YOU MAY ADD YOUR OWN QUESTIONS THAT MAY HAVE COME OUT OF YOUR STUDY EXPERIENCE TOGETHER

EVALUATION/DISCUSSION QUESTIONS

1. **Explain what the writer means when he says, "Baptism marks the Spirit's entry into the Christian's life."**

2. **In order to be saved, which comes first, Baptism, or repentance and confession of faith?**

3. **In what way do you think that Baptism signifies forgiveness?**

---

[15] Jn 16:8

The Holy Spirit and the Effects of Baptism
(Section Two)

1. When we are baptized, it is not the water that saves or washes away our sin

2. As a work of the Holy Spirit, sanctification also begins with our Baptism

3. Forgiveness, justification, regeneration, and sanctification, though distinct, are therefore related terms used to describe the process of our new life in Christ

4. Our renewed life in Christ is the result of our justification through faith and forgiveness, which is our freedom from the guilt and bondage of sin

5. I believe that prevenient grace is God's merciful pre and post intervention in our lives

6. I further believe that prevenient grace is God's proactive action on believers' behalf intended to safeguard our souls from presumptuous sins

7. One of the promises of God is to never leave nor forsake us

8. Here we see an outpouring of God's grace at two levels

—

PAUSE FOR REVIEW

SEE QUESTIONS BELOW TO HELP GUIDE YOUR DISCUSSIONS. YOU MAY ADD YOUR OWN QUESTIONS THAT MAY HAVE COME OUT OF YOUR STUDY EXPERIENCE TOGETHER

EVALUATION/DISCUSSION QUESTION

1. **Since water does not wash away our sins, please share with us how our sins are forgiven**

2. **List and discuss some of the terms used to describe the process of our new life in Christ**

3. **What two terms are used to describe our freedom from the guilt of sin?**

(vii) Baptism: An Opportunity to Grow In Grace
(Section One)

1. Being forgiven, justified, regenerated, and sanctified, and having been baptized do not by any means suggest that we are automatically perfected

2. While we are obviously changed, and while very often the change is sudden, growth in Christ is still a process

3. However, notwithstanding his own deficiencies, Paul also grew to discover the sufficiency of God's grace[16]

4. Faith takes time to develop

5. While in some cases change is truly sudden, for some of us, it takes a while to grow in faith and rid ourselves of bad habits and certain sins that seem to "have our number"

---

[16] 2 Cor 12:9

6. Though we are changed, we still need to resist the temptation to lie, to steal, to gossip, to commit adultery, to commit fornication, to hold grudges, to harbor resentment, to envy others, to practice prejudice and every other form of divine prohibitions

7. Even though as humans we still have the capacity to sin, there should be no desire in us to sin

—

PAUSE FOR REVIEW
SEE QUESTIONS BELOW TO HELP GUIDE YOUR DISCUSSIONS. YOU MAY ADD YOUR OWN QUESTIONS THAT MAY HAVE COME OUT OF YOUR STUDY EXPERIENCE TOGETHER

EVALUATION/DISCUSSION QUESTIONS

1. **Being saved does not mean that we have become perfect. Discuss this statement**

2. **"Faith takes time to develop." Discuss this statement**

3. **Though we are saved, we still have the capacity to sin. Using supporting scriptures where you can, please share with us what you think this statement means**

Baptism: An Opportunity to Grow In Grace
(Section Two)

1. Again, being born-again or regenerated does not mean that we have suddenly arrived at perfection

2. While regeneration marks the beginning of our new journey with God, it is not the end of our growth in Christ

3. Growing up in Christ takes time

4. I have more good news for you!

5. Although we are saved, we are still growing and becoming more like Christ and all that God purposed us to become

6. If you are a newborn in Christ in spiritual training, you can keep in training and develop your faith by aligning yourself with those who are more mature in the Lord

7. Understand then, that God is intent on seeing you through to the completion of His good work in you[17]

8. I have more good news!

9. Assuredly, Baptism marks the beginning of a process of transformation with the divine goal of gradual recovery whereby Christ brings us into the fullness of God[18]

10. As new creatures in Christ, then, the Holy Spirit helps us to be good since we cannot be good all by ourselves

———

[17] Phil 1:6
[18] 2 Pet 3:18

PAUSE FOR REVIEW

SEE QUESTIONS BELOW TO HELP GUIDE YOUR DISCUSSIONS. YOU MAY ADD YOUR OWN QUESTIONS THAT MAY HAVE COME OUT OF YOUR STUDY EXPERIENCE TOGETHER

EVALUATION/DISCUSSION QUESTIONS

1. **"Growing up in Christ takes time." Discuss this statement using examples or sharing personal experience**

2. **Even though God is merciful and His grace abounds, we should not sin in order to receive grace. Discuss this statement using scripture to support your conversation**

3. **As we grow in grace, please share with us some of the best ways to develop our faith**

(viii) Baptism and Our Restored Personhood

1. By the Holy Spirit's entry in our lives at Baptism, we are renewed and our human dignity and personhood are restored by virtue of our new life in Christ

2. Volf observes that "in order to become a person, one must be freed from the restrictions of the biological hypostasis…"[19]

3. Our faithful acceptance of Christ and our desire for Baptism grow out of the recognition that our lives are incomplete, our value inconsequential, and our purpose uncertain, without a spiritual reorientation toward God

4. Through Baptism, the holiness and dignity of God that descended upon Christ in the Jordan, descends upon us by the gift of the Holy Spirit at our Baptism marking the beginning of that process of restoration

---

[19] Mivoslav Volf, <u>After our Likeness: The Church as the Image of the Trinity</u>. Grand Rapids, MI/Cambridge, UK: William B. Eerdmans Publishing Co., 1998: 101

—

PAUSE FOR LESSON REVIEW
QUESTIONS/COMMENTS/CLARIFICATIONS
BREAK INTO GROUP DISCUSSIONS

EVALUATION/DISCUSSION QUESTION

1. **In what ways do you think that Baptism also restores our human dignity?**

2. **"If we are to have liberty in Christ and walk in the dignity of God's holy ways, the natural self needs to be crucified." Using scripture, please discuss and share this perspective with us**

3. **Baptism marks the beginning of the process of our restoration. Do you agree?**

(Selected Liturgical Components of worship, Continues)

D. The Sacrament Of Holy Communion
(Some Scriptures to Consider as we pursue this area of our study are: Mark 14: 22-25; John 6: 11; 1 Corinthians 11: 23-34**)**

(i) Overview
(See general overview of the Sacraments of Holy Baptism and Holy Communion above-under the Sacrament of Holy Baptism)

The objective here is to help us develop an understanding of the meaning and purpose of Holy Communion. I also hope to help us see Holy Communion not merely as an event with historical significance that we cognitively re-member. At a deeper relational level, the celebration of Holy Communion becomes for us an opportunity for our "re-membering" with Christ. Implied by our "re-membering" with Christ is our spiritual reconnection and renewal with the One who died for us. That way, our participation at the Lord's Table becomes a sort of renewal of our membership in the body of Christ as well as the renewing of our covenant relationship with Him. (Some Scriptures to consider as we pursue this area of our study of the Sacrament Holy Communion are: Matthew 26:26-30; Mark 14:22-26; Luke 22:14-20; 1 Corinthians 11:23-34).

—

PAUSE FOR LESSON REVIEW
QUESTIONS/COMMENTS/CLARIFICATIONS
BREAK INTO GROUP DISCUSSIONS

(ii) What is Holy Communion?
(The Passover at a Glance)

1. Holy Communion is the Fellowship Meal of Christ's New Community established by Jesus Christ, signifying a New Covenant (New Testament)

2. This practice of the Passover would become both historicized and traditionalized into the Hebrew and subsequent Jewish culture and tradition under the banner of Israel

3. This typology and the ultimate hope of redemption find fulfillment in Jesus Christ, the true Passover Lamb that takes away the sins of the world[20]

4. During His own ministry, Jesus did in fact participate in several Passovers

5. Jesus' Passover Meal with His disciples and the breaking of the bread and lifting of the cup became new symbols of the new Exodus

6. Holy Communion, like Baptism, is a Sacrament instituted by Jesus at the Last Supper

7. By faith we have resolved that the Sacrament of Holy Communion is the meeting place for renewal and reconnection with Christ for all who believe and confess His Sonship and Lordship

———

[20] Jn 1:29

PAUSE FOR REVIEW

SEE QUESTIONS BELOW TO HELP GUIDE YOUR DISCUSSIONS. YOU MAY
ADD YOUR OWN QUESTIONS THAT MAY HAVE COME OUT OF YOUR STUDY
EXPERIENCE TOGETHER

EVALUATION/DISCUSSION QUESTIONS

1. Why do you think that Holy Communion is often referred to as a fellowship meal?

2. Discuss with each other how the Passover finds its fulfillment in the person of Jesus Christ

3. What practice in the New Testament became the new symbol of the Exodus?

(iii) The Symbolic Value of The Bread and The Wine / Juice

1. The table that we set, along with the elements, the fruits of the vine (the bread and the wine/grape juice), that we put on the Lord's Table, in and by themselves are only of symbolic value

2. The broken bread represents the broken body of Christ

—

PAUSE FOR LESSON REVIEW

QUESTIONS/COMMENTS/CLARIFICATIONS
BREAK INTO GROUP DISCUSSIONS

EVALUATION/DISCUSSION QUESTIONS

1. When do the elements (bread and wine/grape juice) of Holy Communion take on spiritual value or significance?

2. Who is it that ultimately performs the actual consecration of the elements of Holy Communion?

3. In what ways does the broken bread symbolize or represent the broken body of Christ?

(iv) The Holy Spirit at Work in Holy Communion

1. At the most celebrated and venerated of all Christian sacraments, the Holy Spirit is present and actively uniting us with the Father and the Son and each other

2. Because we are sharing in the body and blood of Christ we are essentially sharing in His incarnation and communion with the Father

3. Through the Holy Spirit, God meets us in worship, descends on us at Baptism, communes with us through the sacrament of Holy Communion, and summons us to respond in faith, obedience, and thanksgiving through a committed life in Christ

—

> **PAUSE FOR LESSON REVIEW**
> QUESTIONS/COMMENTS/CLARIFICATIONS
> BREAK INTO GROUP DISCUSSIONS

EVALUATION/DISCUSSION QUESTIONS

1. **Do you agree that Holy Communion is the most celebrated of all Christian sacraments? (Give comparative examples)**

2. **What do you think becoming God-like really means?**

3. **By what means do we obtain the privilege of access to feast at the Lord's Table?**

(v) Holy Communion as Satisfaction for Our Souls

1. As we eat the consecrated bread, the body of Christ, and drink His shed blood symbolized by the grape juice/ wine, we are drawn into the life-giving power of Jesus who died to satisfy the justice of God

2. Holy Communion brings fulfillment and satisfaction to those who hunger and thirst after righteous[21]

———

PAUSE FOR REVIEW

SEE QUESTIONS BELOW TO HELP GUIDE YOUR DISCUSSIONS. YOU MAY ADD YOUR OWN QUESTIONS THAT MAY HAVE COME OUT OF YOUR STUDY EXPERIENCE TOGETHER

EVALUATION/DISCUSSION QUESTIONS

1. **Please share with each other how you think the elements of the bread and grape juice/wine become for us the body and blood of Jesus. Be sure to make notes and report to the rest of us**

2. **Who are those that hunger and thirst after righteousness?**

3. **In what ways do you believe that Holy Communion is a source of spiritual satisfaction?**

(vi) The Spiritually Restorative and Transforming Effects of Holy Communion

1. The restorative and transforming effects of Holy Communion come from our deep sense of the nearness of God and the communion the we have with the Father, Son, and Holy Spirit

2. Holy Communion is restorative because it is a constant reminder to us that we matter to God

---

[21] Mt 5:6

3. Faithful partaking of Holy Communion is spiritually transforming and restorative because Christ, who mediates our worship and our sharing in Holy Communion, also presents us with Himself to the Father by the unitive function of the Holy Spirit

—

PAUSE FOR REVIEW

SEE QUESTIONS BELOW TO HELP GUIDE YOUR DISCUSSIONS. YOU MAY ADD YOUR OWN QUESTIONS THAT MAY HAVE COME OUT OF YOUR STUDY EXPERIENCE TOGETHER

EVALUATION/DISCUSSION QUESTIONS

1. **In what ways is Holy Communion a constant reminder that we matter to God?**

2. **Discuss among yourselves how you think that Holy Communion is spiritually transforming and restorative**

3. **Based on your understanding of scripture and the ascension of Jesus, discuss amongst yourselves how it is that Jesus is able to present us with Himself to the Father. Be prepared to share your findings with the rest of us**

(vii) How Holy Communion Redefines Who We Are In Christ

1. As already stated in the case of our baptism, as a result of our communion with God, our personhood and eternal value can no longer be defined by human divisions of race, gender, nationality, and social positions

2. Our human differences of race, nationality, ethnicity, and social standings no longer matter because through Jesus, we have all become adopted sons and daughters of God

MADE FOR ETERNITY · STUDY OUTLINE

3. What this means for us who are adopted by God is that God, not us, and not sin, God alone has authority and dominion over us

4. Being adopted by God also means that all that He has is ours and all that we have become we owe to Him

—

> ## PAUSE FOR REVIEW
> SEE QUESTIONS BELOW TO HELP GUIDE YOUR DISCUSSIONS. YOU MAY ADD YOUR OWN QUESTIONS THAT MAY HAVE COME OUT OF YOUR STUDY EXPERIENCE TOGETHER

EVALUATION/DISCUSSION QUESTIONS

1. **In your own words, how do you think that participation in Holy Communion draws us into the life giving power of Jesus Christ?**

2. **Based on your personal experience, does Holy Communion make a difference to you, and how has sharing in the Lord's Supper or Holy Communion, impacted your life?**

3. **According to the author, "As a result of our communion with God, our personhood and eternal value can no longer be defined by human divisions of race, gender, nationality, and social position." Do you agree? Giving examples, use scripture to support your view**

4. **Using scripture, please discuss in your groups and share with the rest of us your understanding of the significance of our adoption by God the Father**

5. **As you break into small groups, discuss and then share with us how Holy Communion redefines who we are in Christ**

(viii) Holy Communion as Re-presenting and "Re-membering With" Christ

1. On every occasion that we come to the Lord's Table for Holy Communion, the Holy Spirit ministers Christ to us

2. The work of Christ on the cross that we commemorate through Holy Communion is not just a moment in time that we remember; it is an experience that we live

3. When we come to the Lord's Table, then, we do not do so merely to remember a date and time in history

4. Holy Communion is therefore more than the celebration or memory of an event of spiritual significance or historical proportion

5. Furthermore, when we speak of Holy Communion as a memory, it is not merely a cognitive recalling of an event

—

PAUSE FOR REVIEW

SEE QUESTIONS BELOW TO HELP GUIDE YOUR DISCUSSIONS. YOU MAY
ADD YOUR OWN QUESTIONS THAT MAY HAVE COME OUT OF YOUR STUDY
EXPERIENCE TOGETHER

EVALUATION/DISCUSSION QUESTIONS

1. **Please share with us your understanding of Holy Communion as a re-presenting of and a re-membering with Christ**

2. **Discuss the view that Holy Communion is more than the remembrance of a moment in history**

3. **Through Holy Communion, the Holy Spirit re-establishes our union with God. Discuss**

(ix) Holy Communion and the Forgiveness of Our Sins

1. The universal invitation to the Lord's Table was given by Christ the night before He was offered up as the Sacrificial Lamb

2. The invitation to the Lord's Table is still a call to repentance and at the same time an invitation to receive forgiveness and atonement

3. Holy Communion is an affirmation of our forgiveness and reconciliation with God and each other

4. By our sharing in the Holy Communion, and by the illuminating Spirit of grace, all generations of the faithful and expectant Church have learned to see and know themselves to be a people whose sins Jesus nailed to the cross, not in part but the whole. Hallelujah!

—

PAUSE FOR REVIEW
SEE QUESTIONS BELOW TO HELP GUIDE YOUR DISCUSSIONS. YOU MAY ADD YOUR OWN QUESTIONS THAT MAY HAVE COME OUT OF YOUR STUDY EXPERIENCE TOGETHER

EVALUATION/DISCUSSION QUESTIONS

1. **Using the statements of liturgical invitations, share with us in what ways you think that the invitation to the Lord's Table is a call to repentance as well as a call for fellowship and communion**

2. **Do you agree that our faithful sharing of Holy Communion is a sort of affirmation of our forgiveness and reconciliation with God and each other? If so, in what ways?**

3. **Take a moment to share with us your understanding of the Holy Spirit as the illuminating Spirit of grace**

(x) Holy Communion as an Opportunity for Thanksgiving

1. Let us quickly recap what Holy Communion is for us

2. When we consider all these and other benefits of the Passions of Christ, Holy Communion presents us with the opportunity to recount the great deeds of God with profound gratitude

3. We are thankful because Jesus, having secured our salvation through His death, has given us the assurance of victory over death by His resurrection

—

> **PAUSE FOR LESSON REVIEW**
> **QUESTIONS/COMMENTS/CLARIFICATIONS**
> **BREAK INTO GROUP DISCUSSIONS**

EVALUATION/DISCUSSION QUESTIONS

1. **Please take a moment to share with us what you have learned about Holy Communion so far**

2. **In your own words, please share with us how Holy Communion is an opportunity for thanksgiving**

3. **What in particular are you personally thankful for?**

(Selected Liturgical Components of worship, Continues)

E. The Doxology

(i) What Is The Doxology?

1. The doxology is a statement of glory ascribed to God

2. We also have what are known as the Lesser and Greater Doxologies

3. The doxology is fundamental to Christian worship because it is a constant reminder to us of the majesty, power, and glory of God

4. The doctrinal affirmations of the doxology also help in our understanding of how worship becomes a dialogue that connects us to God and God to us

5. Doxologies are useful for the Christian worshipper at five levels of theological understanding

6. The ultimate liturgical and theological objective of the doxology is to empower believers to reach up to God through understanding and therefore with purposeful praise

7. In worship, when used in the preliminary or opening stages of formal worship, the doxology is an announcement of celebration

—

PAUSE FOR REVIEW

SEE QUESTIONS BELOW TO HELP GUIDE YOUR DISCUSSIONS. YOU MAY
ADD YOUR OWN QUESTIONS THAT MAY HAVE COME OUT OF YOUR STUDY
EXPERIENCE TOGETHER

EVALUATION/DISCUSSION QUESTIONS

1. How has today's lesson helped your understanding of the liturgy of worship?

2. Of the different segments of the liturgy discussed, what components of the liturgy did you find most informative and why?

3. What do you think is the value of the liturgy in worship?

4. What is the purpose of the doxology and how does the doxology help your understanding of praise in worship?

5. The liturgy of worship does not end with the singing of the doxology and the pronouncement of the benediction. What does this mean to you?

6. What recommendation would you personally make to help inform this congregation about worship?

(ii) Living Doxological Lives
The Liturgical and Doxological Nature of Christian Living
(Section One)

1. Living doxological lives is really about practicing what we preach

2. Knowledge of God ought to cultivate in us the desire to bring continuous praise to His name by the way we live our lives in the world

3. Our daily liturgy is the way we live our lives as beneficiaries of God's goodness and as witnesses to His mercy and grace

4. While liturgical observations are not necessarily indicators of holiness, proper observation and practice of the purpose of the liturgy may induce holiness

5. Participation in the liturgical practices of worship as a custom not only has faith and tutorial values, it also has behavioral values for life

---

PAUSE FOR LESSON REVIEW
QUESTIONS/COMMENTS/CLARIFICATIONS
BREAK INTO GROUP DISCUSSIONS

EVALUATION/DISCUSSION QUESTIONS

1. **What do you think the writer means when he says, "Living doxological lives is really about practicing what we preach?"**

2. **Make and discuss a list of ways that we can bring glory to God by the way we live our lives in the world**

3. **In what ways do you think that liturgical observation can induce holiness?**

4. **In what ways do you think faith has tutorial value and how can such values affect our behavior?**

Living Doxological Lives
The Liturgical and Doxological Nature of Christian Living
(Section Two)

1. We begin to lead doxological lives when, having learned the ways of God, we are moved by what we learn about God to display those ways in our dealings with others

2. The liturgy of worship is not only to be recited, it is to inform our faith, inspire our hope, and influence our actions

3. We live doxological lives when we are empowered by the Holy Spirit to effectively and faithfully participate in God's redemptive and liberating acts in the world

4. The community of faith, the Church, is not only a worshipping community as it relates to formal worship; it is also a working community that should be actively seeking to bring glory to God by the way we live and behave in the world

5. The human pursuit of holiness is ignited by our awareness of the holiness of God which is grounded in worship, and finds active expressions through our intentional living out the liturgy of worship in the world through acts of righteousness

6. Without our intentional pursuit of active service we run the risk of worshipping only in words and not with active, expectant, and participative faith

7. True worship never really ends

8. Our doxological living is only made possible by the empowering Spirit of grace

9. From the narrow and "secured" confines of our places of worship, God has called and anointed us to go forth into the world to live doxological lives

10. Speaking of the true meaning of Christianity and a manifested doxological life style, the story of the Good Samaritan in Luke 10:25-37 comes to mind

———

PAUSE FOR LESSON REVIEW
QUESTIONS/COMMENTS/CLARIFICATIONS
BREAK INTO GROUP DISCUSSIONS

EVALUATION/DISCUSSION QUESTIONS

1. **In what ways can our understanding of the ways of God contribute to our living doxological lives?**

2. **In what ways do you think the liturgy of worship can inform our faith, inspire our hope, and influence our holy actions?**

3. **"True worship never really ends." Discuss this statement giving examples**

Living Doxological Lives
The Liturgical and Doxological Nature of Christian Living
(Section Three)

1. There, on that unforgiving Jericho Road, the doxology of praise through service of love and mercy spilled over from an unlikely source

2. On the Jericho road, this "certain man" laid there after being beaten, robbed, and left half dead

3. Perhaps the priest and the Levite convinced themselves that the situation was none of their business

4. The unlikely source of blessing and compassion, a certain Samaritan, came along that same Jericho Road

5. The story of the Good Samaritan was prompted by a young lawyer seeking to justify himself in a previous discourse with Jesus when he asked, "...Who is my neighbor?"

6. Someone, undoubtedly a beneficiary of grace and mercy, once testified:

—

PAUSE FOR LESSON REVIEW
QUESTIONS/COMMENTS/CLARIFICATIONS
BREAK INTO GROUP DISCUSSIONS

EVALUATION/DISCUSSION QUESTIONS

1. **How did the Good Samaritan demonstrate the doxology of praise through service?**

2. **Who is our neighbor?**

3. **Giving examples, make a list of ways that you think we as persons and a church can be more neighborly**

Living Doxological Lives
The Liturgical and Doxological Nature of Christian Living
(Section Four)

1. The story of the Good Samaritan is an indictment

2. A doxological life is a life that is dedicated to the lifting up of the fallen and downtrodden who, in not so "secure" a world, have been stricken and beaten down by misfortune and sin and need to be rescued and restored

3. If, on your way to heaven, you see others standing by the road with life's heavy load, it is your Christian duty to give a helping hand

4. On that Jericho Road, God did send help from likely sources to help the man beaten up and left half-dead in the form of two religious persons and worshippers, a priest and a Levite

5. Christ has taught us that love for God should not be restricted to formal worship alone, but needs to extend to serving those who are deprived, hurt, excluded, abandoned, and avoided by others

6. In worship and daily living, our doxology ought to become continuous confession, adoration, thanksgiving, devotion, and service

7. The singing of the doxology and the pronouncement of the benediction do not signify the dismissal or conclusion of worship

8. As worship spills over in our daily lives and encompasses our daily activities then, a doxological life calls the Christian to shine his/her light in a dark and lonely world

9. To conclude that the celebration of the liturgy of worship ends at the singing of the doxology and the pronouncement of the benediction is to mummify worship

10. Worship is continuous

11. Moving from the liturgy of worship to the liturgy of life and service is not a transition into a different compartment of our lives

---

PAUSE FOR REVIEW

SEE QUESTIONS BELOW TO HELP GUIDE YOUR DISCUSSIONS. YOU MAY ADD YOUR OWN QUESTIONS THAT MAY HAVE COME OUT OF YOUR STUDY EXPERIENCE TOGETHER

EVALUATION/DISCUSSION QUESTIONS

1. What are some of the trappings of life that people sometimes become burdened by?

2. From the point of view of service and praise, how would you define your Christian duties or responsibilities?

3. In what ways is lifting up the fallen and downtrodden a form of honoring and giving glory to God?

4. What are the similarities and differences between the liturgy of worship and the liturgy of service? Do you think one is more important than the other? Why?

5. Please share with us what you understand by worship that spills over into our daily lives

6. According to the author, "To conclude that the celebration of the liturgy of worship ends at the singing of the doxology and the pronouncement of the benediction is to mummify worship." In what ways do you think we mummify worship?

7. "Worship never ends." What are your thoughts and what excites you most about serving God in the world?

CHAPTER FIVE

CHRISTIAN MISSION

Devotional Exercise
    Welcome/Greetings
    Sharing of prayer concerns
    Prayer
    Hymn(s) of the day
    Scripture selection(s) for today

Prayer:
    Heavenly Father, I praise You today because You are God and worthy of praise. As I contemplate going out into the world today, give me the desire and develop in me a deep sense of commitment to serve you through serving others. Empower me so that I may willingly offer myself in service to my fellow humans as I witness to Your glory in the world. By Your indwelling Spirit, ready me I pray to face the challenges and accept the opportunities You present me to reach up to You by reaching out to others. O Lord God eternal, please empty me of myself and all contemplations of my own desires and accomplishments. Ready me with Your quickening power, surround me with Your presence, and infuse me with Your grace so that I leave nothing undone that You require of me today. Help me to put others and their needs and aspirations before me and my own needs, and to put You always before all. Grant me the boldness to speak Your Word as I go forth to make disciples for Christ. Lord, I declare my love for You. Move me by Your Holy Spirit to declare my love to my brothers and sisters through the demonstration of mercy and justice before those that I encounter today. As I interact with others in my service to You in the world, help me by Your Spirit to align my actions in the world with the words that I have confessed in worship, so that I may be fully Yours in all that I do and say. For these and all of Your mercies I pray in the name of Jesus, Amen!

Scripture: Isaiah 49:3-4; Luke 4:18-19; 24:47-49; Acts 2:1-4

Hymns:
    "A Charge To Keep I Have"
    "Come Holy Ghost, Our Souls Inspire" \
    "How Shall They Hear The Word of God?"
    "Go Make All Disciples"
    "We Have A Story To Tell"

"Pass It On"
"Spirit Of The Living God"
"Breathe On Me Breath Of God"
"Where He Leads Me I Will Follow"
"This Little Light Of Mine"

Objective(s)
To help us:

- Develop a practical understanding of Christian mission
- Understand the continuous relations between worship and Christian mission
- Understand how worship equips us for Christian mission
- Understand the role and presence of the Holy Spirit for Christian mission
- Develop an awareness of the practice of Christian mission as a source of spiritual transformation
- Develop an awareness of the liturgy of worship and the liturgy of mission as transforming agents

1. OVERVIEW

This chapter is an examination of Christian mission. Attention will be given to an examination of the dual and continuous relations between Christian worship and Christian mission. The coming and necessity of the Holy Spirit for mission will be discussed. The Holy Spirit, as we shall see, is God's gift of power for Christian mission and witness. Consequently, Christian mission is the working of the Holy Spirit. Using scripture references, we will promote the belief that God is a missional God. As a missional God, He is the God that sends. As a consequence and an imperative, our holy and worshipful confrontation or encounter with God in worship becomes an opportunity for our sanctification and empowerment for mission. How the conviction of faith developed in worship spills over into corresponding demonstrations of faith through Christian mission; how participation in Christian mission leads to the spiritual formation or shaping of the Christian's life, character, and growth in Christ, and the importance of building relationships for doing Christian mission, will also be critical components of this level of our examination.

2. WHAT IS CHRISTIAN MISSION?

1. Christian Mission is faith in action

2. God's mission began in creation

3. Our engagement in Christian mission means that we are God's witnesses to the world

4. Christian mission is God making visible in the world, through our proclamation and service, His Word, actions, and intention to lift up fallen humanity

—

PAUSE FOR LESSON REVIEW
QUESTIONS/COMMENTS/CLARIFICATIONS

EVALUATION/DISCUSSION QUESTIONS

1. **Giving examples, please share with us how you think Christian Mission is faith in action**

2. **What does the writer mean when he says, "God's mission began in creation?"**

3. **As God's witnesses in the world, how can we make visible in the word and actions of God?**

3. THE RELATIONS BETWEEN WORSHIP AND CHRISTIAN MISSION (SECTION ONE)

1. The primary functions of the Church are worship and mission

2. Worship therefore becomes a sort of precursor of a movement in which God shakes us free from all the constraints of life and our own cares and preoccupations, so that His power and grace may equip us for Christian mission and the giving of ourselves to the world

3. From a Biblical perspective, to profess Christ through worship and not live Christ in the world makes that profession false

4. As we encounter God in worship and in life, we are empowered by that very encounter to be witnesses

5. I am certainly not contending that worship is to be used as a tool for preparing us for mission

6. Every true worshipper ought to be a true public witness

7. This dual purpose of worship and mission may be best understood as a sort of double or shared expressions of God's love in worship through praise and in the world through active Christian mission that brings Him glory

---

PAUSE FOR LESSON REVIEW
QUESTIONS/COMMENTS/CLARIFICATIONS
BREAK INTO GROUP DISCUSSIONS

EVALUATION/DISCUSSION QUESTIONS

1. **In what way does worship prepare you for Christian mission?**

2. **Take a few moments to discuss the primary functions of the church. Be sure to measure our effectiveness as individual worshippers as well as a collective body, the church**

3. **In your own words share with us your thinking concerning our profession of faith and the practicing of our faith**

4. **According to the writer, "Every true worshipper ought to be a true public witness." Do you think that we can be balanced Christian persons or congregation if we worship but do not go out into the world to serve?**

5. What are your thoughts on today's lesson?

The Relations Between Worship And Christian Mission (Section Two)

1. To cultivate disparity between our worship in word and our worship through service and Christian mission is to create an unhealthy imbalance between what we confess in the formal worship and what we do and practice in the world

2. As Christians, we are called to be both worshippers and witnesses

3. Worship and mission are not discontinuous; they are a continuous duet and a perpetual dance

4. In worship, then, we sing God's praise, and in mission the liturgy of work becomes sweet music to our souls because we rejoice in the fact that God is making use of us

5. Full and complete Christian discipleship calls for the incorporation of both worship and Christian mission

6. Mission is an imperative extension of our worship

—

PAUSE FOR REVIEW

SEE QUESTIONS BELOW TO HELP GUIDE YOUR DISCUSSIONS. YOU MAY
ADD YOUR OWN QUESTIONS THAT MAY HAVE COME OUT OF YOUR STUDY
EXPERIENCE TOGETHER

EVALUATION/DISCUSSION QUESTIONS

1. What are some of the ways that we can create disparity between worship in word and worship through service?

2. Please take a moment to discuss how worship and mission may be considered a continuous duet and a perpetual dance

3. How has this lesson changed your understanding of Christian mission?

THE RELATIONS BETWEEN WORSHIP AND CHRISTIAN MISSION (SECTION THREE)

1. In Christ, word (ethical presupposing) and work (ethical consequences) are inseparable

2. To affirm our love for God without demonstrative faith, or faith that works, is to promote both lazy as well as cheap grace

3. Every Sabbath, the historical Christ entered the synagogue to worship the Father and departed to lift up the fallen and broken remnant of humanity

4. If indeed we are followers of Christ, we ought to be vehicles for the living presence of Christ in the Church as well as in the world

5. As Christians, then, we show love for God at two levels of human existence

6. Through Christian mission we become Christ to the world

7. Like the man in the above story, we need to exemplify Christ in the world

8. Because worship and mission are not distinct, we are not only praisers that eat at the Lord's Table and find comfortable places to rest when the worship service is "over." We are also praisers that work

9. If the world is to take the Church seriously, the Church needs to live up to the demands of the Gospel imperative

10. The objective of worship and mission is for us to intentionally share in all that Christ the Son has done in worship and service to bring glory to God

11. In worship we celebrate God's forgiveness and in mission we extend that forgiveness to our brothers and sisters

12. Every Christian has his/her liturgy to perform within the congregation and outside of it

———

PAUSE FOR REVIEW

SEE QUESTIONS BELOW TO HELP GUIDE YOUR DISCUSSIONS. YOU MAY
ADD YOUR OWN QUESTIONS THAT MAY HAVE COME OUT OF YOUR STUDY
EXPERIENCE TOGETHER

EVALUATION/DISCUSSION QUESTIONS

1. What do you understand by the term "continuous worship of God" beyond the Sunday morning worship service?

2. List two ways that this lesson has helped you develop a better understanding of the continuous process of worship as it relates to mission

3. Based on today's lesson, in what ways do you think we can best reflect Christ in the world?

4. Are you satisfied with your level of commitment to Christian mission? What adjustments are you willing to make in order to commit

5. In what ways do you think you can improve?

6. According to the author, "Every Christian has his/her liturgy to perform both within the congregation and outside of it." Explain

7. List three things that you are prepared to do this week to demonstrate your commitment to Christ through mission

4. THE COMING AND NECESSITY OF THE HOLY SPIRIT FOR MISSION (SECTION ONE)

1. Let us first attempt to address the matter of the person of the Holy Spirit. Who is the Holy Spirit?

2. As the third Person in the Godhead, the Holy Spirit has divine attributes

3. The Holy Spirit, contrary to what some believe, is not a New Testament phenomenon

4. On the Day of Pentecost, the Holy Spirit descended upon, and entered the life of the Early Church in a new and powerful way

5. In Christian mission, our primary goal is to win souls for Jesus as we encourage the unchurched and the unredeemed to believe in Christ for salvation

6. Through Christian mission, God has called and empowered us to shine our light in the world

7. The Holy Spirit, as the Spirit of illumination, is the pervasive light of God in the world

8. Since the goal of Christian mission is to make disciples for Christ by bringing people into awareness and saving faith in Jesus and fellowship with God, we essentially have to witness to lost and broken people

9. The realization that we are saved through Christ and empowered by the Holy Spirit to do the work of God in the world does not mean that we should exalt ourselves above the people that we think are not saved

10. As a gift to us, the Holy Spirit turns our attention from self and redirects our lives and attention toward God and those we are called to serve

11. In our service to the world, our goal should never be to win the world for our credit, to fulfill the local church mission drive, or to meet goals for percentage membership increases for the year in our local churches

—

PAUSE FOR LESSON REVIEW
QUESTIONS/COMMENTS/CLARIFICATIONS
BREAK INTO GROUP DISCUSSIONS

EVALUATION/DISCUSSION QUESTIONS

1. **Who is the Holy Spirit?**

2. **Why do you think it was necessary for the Holy Spirit to come?**

3. **List three ways by which the Holy Spirit helps us to carry out Christian mission**

4. **How do you witness for Christ in the world?**

5. **Please share with us how you have benefitted from today's lessons**

THE COMING AND NECESSITY OF THE HOLY SPIRIT FOR MISSION (SECTION TWO)

1. In mission, without the Holy Spirit imparting Christ to us and to those to whom we witness, we would focus on ourselves, our wisdom, our experience, our abilities, and our expertise

2. When we believe it is our ability that matters most whether in worship or in mission, "we violate the holiness of the Spirit by resisting Him in His self-effacing office and confusing Him with our own spirits"[22]

3. Obedience is important for Christian mission because it makes Christian mission effectual

4. The faith that we have in Christ and the task of mission that we have been given, are gifts of the Holy Spirit

5. God gives the Holy Spirit to us because without the Holy Spirit, our mission, like our worship without the Spirit, would become, at best, our own inventions and works, and not the works and manifestations of God

6. As we serve God through Christian mission in the world, despite the challenges and sometimes the discouragement that accompany such mission, the Holy Spirit encourages our hearts with the guarantee of God's eternal promise[23]

7. To that extent, Christian mission has eschatological significance

—

---

[22] Torrance, "Come Creator Spirit…," 142

[23] 2 Cor 1:22; 5:5; Eph 4:30

PAUSE FOR REVIEW
BREAK INTO GROUPS FOR DISCUSSION ON THE ROLE
OF THE HOLY SPIRIT IN OUR LIVES AND MISSION

EVALUATION/DISCUSSION QUESTIONS

1. **"When we believe it is our ability that matters most whether in worship or in mission, we violate the holiness of the Spirit…" Discuss this statement in light of worship and mission as gifts from God**

2. **Discuss with each other why you think obedience is important in carrying out Christian mission**

3. **Can we do God's work without God's help?**

5. THE HOLY SPIRIT AS THE GIFT OF POWER FOR CHRISTIAN MISSION

1. God has given us the gift of the Holy Spirit to empower us for ministry

2. No ministry should be attempted without the anointing of the Holy Spirit

3. God has given us the gift of the Holy Spirit so that we may become empowered and effective participants in the ministry of Christ

4. Human wisdom, strength, and ability, alone, cannot accomplish the work of God

5. As our gift of power, the Holy Spirit is authorized to draw our attention to Christ and furnish us with the gift of impartation

6. As our worship is first the worship of the Son to the Father before it is ours, so our mission and witness are the mission of the Holy Spirit before they are our mission and witness[24]

7. On the one hand, then, God deserves our love and demands our service. On the other hand, God is the source of our ability to both love and serve Him

8. In mission, the Holy Spirit is for us the life sustaining power of God

—

```
┌─────────────────────────────────────────┐
│        PAUSE FOR LESSON REVIEW           │
├─────────────────────────────────────────┤
│   QUESTIONS/COMMENTS/CLARIFICATIONS      │
├─────────────────────────────────────────┤
│     BREAK INTO GROUP DISCUSSIONS         │
└─────────────────────────────────────────┘
```

EVALUATION/DISCUSSION QUESTIONS

1. **Why should we depend on the wisdom of the Holy Spirit to guide us in life and in mission?**

2. **How is our witness of Christ in the world first the witness of the Holy Spirit?**

3. **As in the case of worship, what happens to our witness/mission without the Holy Spirit?**

4. **Do you think it is ok to pat ourselves on the back when we accomplish something through the ministries of the church?**

5. **What are your thoughts on the matter of the role and impact of the Holy Spirit on Christian mission?**

---

[24] 1 Jn 5:6-10a

6. GOD IS A MISSIONAL GOD:
CONFRONTED AND SANCTIFIED FOR MISSION
(SECTION ONE)

1. God is a missional God because He is the God that sends

2. A new mission is always preceded by a new vision, a restored consciousness or a new awareness of God

3. We should never take God's self-disclosure for granted

4. Since the Christian life is a lifelong journey of transformation and repositioning by the Holy Spirit of grace, the question that immediately confronts us is: "What is the Christian's response to God who confronts us with His grace?"

5. In the fourth chapter of the Gospel of John, it was the Samaritan woman's encounter with Christ that led her to depart with a burning desire to share the good news of her face-to-face encounter with the Christ

—

PAUSE FOR REVIEW
SEE QUESTIONS BELOW TO HELP GUIDE YOUR DISCUSSIONS. YOU MAY ADD YOUR OWN QUESTIONS THAT MAY HAVE COME OUT OF YOUR STUDY EXPERIENCE TOGETHER

EVALUATION/DISCUSSION QUESTIONS

1. **Using scripture to support your position, please share with us in what ways God is a missional God**

2. **Why do you think God reveals Himself to us?**

3. How does God's self-disclosure to us move us to proclaim Him to the world?

4. **Using the encounter of the woman of Samaria with Jesus, and giving biblical examples, please discuss and be prepared to share with us your view of women in ministry**

GOD IS A MISSIONAL GOD
CONFRONTED AND SANCTIFIED FOR MISSION
(SECTION TWO)

1. Christian believers are motivated to become witnesses for Christ in the world because what we know about God is what we have encountered and experienced in Christ

2. We must proclaim and therefore release what God has deposited in us because we do not have the capacity to contain God or what He has deposited in us

3. God confronts and reveals Himself to us for a reason

———

PAUSE FOR REVIEW
SEE QUESTIONS BELOW TO HELP GUIDE YOUR DISCUSSIONS. YOU MAY ADD YOUR OWN QUESTIONS THAT MAY HAVE COME OUT OF YOUR STUDY EXPERIENCE TOGETHER

EVALUATION/DISCUSSION QUESTIONS

1. **Using your understanding of the life and ministry of Jesus, share with us what motivates you to become witnesses for Christ in the world**

2. **How do you feel about God revealing Himself to you and making use of you in His mission to redeem the world?**

3. **Using scripture and personal experiences, please share with us how you think God has furnished us with the evidence of His existence**

GOD IS A MISSIONAL GOD
CONFRONTED AND SANCTIFIED FOR MISSION
(SECTION THREE)

1. Our encounter with God is contagious by design and every encounter with God is a formula for spreading a compelling testimony

2. Our encounter with God is for the conviction and building up of our faith and witness

3. Having encountered God, and having been transformed by His redeeming grace in Christ Jesus, through mission, we become demonstrative evidence of His grace in the world

4. Since what we are called to do is a gift, we must be careful not to think that we are the ones changing the world

5. To restrict the working out of God's purpose to a particular place or surrounding, such as where we regularly gather to worship, would be a presumptuous attempt to restrict and domesticate the operation of the Holy Spirit

6. As we carry out mission with Christ, we need to urgently recognize that people outside the conventional church also have a deep spiritual hunger

7. Since Christian Mission emerges from an assignment that springs out of our recognition, interpretation, and application of our encounter with God, our missional engagements ought rightly to give us a worldview

8. We are confronted so that we may be equipped to go forth into the world with a message of redemption and hope

9. Have you encountered the risen Christ?

PAUSE FOR REVIEW

SEE QUESTIONS BELOW TO HELP GUIDE YOUR DISCUSSIONS. YOU MAY ADD YOUR OWN QUESTIONS THAT MAY HAVE COME OUT OF YOUR STUDY EXPERIENCE TOGETHER

EVALUATION/DISCUSSION QUESTIONS

1. According the author, "Our encounter with God is contagious by design and every encounter with God is a formulation for a compelling testimony." Explain this statement using the prophet Jeremiah and the Apostle Paul as your reference points

2. Do you agree that our encounter with God is for the conviction and building up of our faith? What examples from the Bible can you draw on to support your position?

3. How do you think we as Christians can be demonstrative evidence of God's grace in the world?

4. Do you agree that there is a deep spiritual hunger in people outside the conventional church? If yes, or no, please say how and what the role of the church is in satisfying that hunger

5. Please share your thoughts with us regarding today's topic

7. PRACTICING CHRISTIAN MISSION AND THE SHAPING OF THE CHRISTIAN LIFE

A. Christian Mission as Character Building and Spiritual Formation

1. Our Christian mission, much like Christian worship, helps in the formation of our spirituality

2. Practicing Christian mission helps us our spiritual formation at two levels

3. In the mission field where real mission takes place, character is also molded

4. Transformation happens in mission when the Holy Spirit opens our awareness to the realization that we are of value to God

5. The knowledge that we belong to God and are sharing in the ministry of Christ is powerful source of spiritual transformation and opportunity to grow in Christ

6. Christian mission shapes the Christian life because wherever and whenever the Holy Spirit of God is present and working in us, change is inevitable

PAUSE FOR REVIEW
SEE QUESTIONS BELOW TO HELP GUIDE YOUR DISCUSSIONS. YOU MAY ADD YOUR OWN QUESTIONS THAT MAY HAVE COME OUT OF YOUR STUDY EXPERIENCE TOGETHER

EVALUATION/DISCUSSION QUESTIONS

1. **"As true worship does not leave us unchanged, committed participation in Christian mission does not leave us unchanged." Discuss this statement showing how the practice of Christian can change our lives**

2. **Giving examples, please tell us in your own words how, and in what ways, the mission field can become a source of character building**

3. **Drawing on Romans 12: 2 and the content of today's lesson, take a moment to share with us how you think awareness of God helps in the reshaping of our thinking**

B. Christian Mission and the Building of Relationships: The Four Levels of Interrelated Christian Relationships

1. Christian mission is built on four levels of interrelated Christian networking and relationships

2. As we engage in Christian mission, our growth in Christ is practically facilitated by Christian networking and relationships

3. **Level One:** Where the Shepherd is Shepherded

4. **Level Two**: Where We Participate in Missions with Our Peers

5. **Level Three**: Where We Shepherd and Tend to Others

6. **Level Four**: Where the Sheep Produce More Sheep

7. The point to remember about these levels of relationships is that when we are engaged in ministry with Christ, we are better and stronger together than we are apart

—

PAUSE FOR REVIEW
SEE QUESTIONS BELOW TO HELP GUIDE YOUR DISCUSSIONS. YOU MAY ADD YOUR OWN QUESTIONS THAT MAY HAVE COME OUT OF YOUR STUDY EXPERIENCE TOGETHER

EVALUATION/DISCUSSION QUESTIONS

1. **Why do you think it is important to build Christian networks or relationships in order to effectively carry out Christian mission?**

2. **Please take a moment to reflect on and discuss with each other the four levels of relationship in Christian mission**

3. **What are your thoughts on the contributions of networking, internet, and social media to the carrying out of Christian mission?**

CHAPTER SIX

DIVERSITY AND CHRISTIAN MISSION

Devotional Exercise

Welcome/Greetings

Sharing of prayer concerns

Prayer

Hymn(s) of the day

Scripture selection(s) for today

Prayer:

Merciful and loving God, equip me as I go forth in the world to serve Your people. Give me the grace and a heart filled with love so that I may accept and love all persons without regard for what they look like or where they come from. My heart is opened and my mind is fixed on bringing glory to You today. Empower me therefore to embrace the differences that You have created so that I may celebrate the richness of your diverse world and diverse people. This I pray in the precious name of Jesus, Amen!

Hymns:

"All Things Bright And Beautiful"

"All People That On Earth Do Dwell"

"We Are One In The Spirit'

"When We All Get To Heaven"

"Make Us One Lord"

Scriptures: Jn 17:20-23; 1 Cor 12; Eph 4:1-16

Objectives:

To aid our understanding of:

- The phenomenon of diversity
- The prevailing presence of diversity in churches and health care facilities
- Methodologies for responding to, appreciating, and caring for a diverse people
- How a diverse God is working in and through a diverse people to bring them into His diverse kingdom

1. WHAT IS DIVERSITY?

1. Diversity is the existence of differences encompassing a rich array of religious, national, ethnic, gender, cultural, age, and generational variables

2. Diversity is a biblically endorsed phenomenon

3. Not everyone is open to or willing to recognize, accept, and honor the changing trends, richness, and value of diversity in our society today

4. If we desire to become culturally relevant, however, diversity is a reality that ought to be acknowledged, embraced, and promoted

5. As Christians, we are essentially a diverse people

PAUSE FOR LESSON REVIEW
QUESTIONS/COMMENTS/CLARIFICATIONS
BREAK INTO GROUP DISCUSSIONS

EVALUATION/DISCUSSION QUESTIONS

1. **Please list and discuss the different variables associated with diversity**

2. **What does the Bible teach us about diversity?**

3. **Why do you think some people are not as accepting of diversity (in society, the workplace, health care facilities, and the church)?**

4. **What are some things that we can do to embrace and honor diversity in our attempts to glorify God?**

5. **Giving examples, please share with us the ways that you think God and the kingdom of God are diverse?**

2. THE MISSION OF THE CHURCH IN A DIVERSE/PLURALISTIC SOCIETY

1. A diverse and pluralistic society is one in which we have people with different ethnic origins, cultural orientations, religious views, and political preferences

2. The vocation of the Church in a pluralistic society is to mediate the reconciling love of God and create and nurture inclusive communities that live under the power and authority of the resurrected Christ

3. As the church is enriched by the diverse manifestations of God, so should our witness and service be enriched by our embracing of the oneness of a diverse humanity

4. Our failure to adapt, without compromising our faith and loyalty first to God, may render us left behind and culturally irrelevant

5. Diversity is an important component of worship, mission, and life

6. In worship, wherever Christians are gathered in the spirit of oneness, it should always be a place and an opportunity for people to bring their entire existence and diverse experiences to the worship of a diverse God

7. Regardless of who we are, what denominations we belong to, what schools we and our children go to, what color our skins are, what neighborhoods we come from, none of us has a monopoly on God

8. God's kingdom is a diverse kingdom

9. Because of the human failure to accept and celebrate differences, some of us are still afraid to "go through Samaria"

10. According to Scripture, Jesus was on His way to Galilee but felt an urgent need to go through Samaria[25]

11. Jesus Christ journeyed and tarried and gave of Himself in places and to people where it was neither customary nor safe to do so

12. We must not wait until we get to heaven to honor diversity

———

| PAUSE FOR LESSON REVIEW |
| QUESTIONS/COMMENTS/CLARIFICATIONS |
| BREAK INTO GROUP DISCUSSIONS |

EVALUATION/DISCUSSION QUESTIONS

1. **In your opinion, what do you think is the vocation (mission) of the church and how effectively is the church carrying out that vocation?**

2. **In what ways can we as persons and a church be considered irrelevant?**

---

[25] Jn 4:1-26

3. **Given that the church is becoming increasingly diverse, do you think we can effectively serve or meet the needs of diverse persons without understanding the diverse social concerns and life experiences that they bring to the worship encounter?**

4. **Because of the human failure to accept and celebrate differences, some of us are still afraid to "go through Samaria." Discuss this statement in light of socio-economic differences, social stratification, and neighborhood divides**

5. **Keeping diversity in mind, how do you think we can make the world a reflection of heaven?**

3. DIVERSITY AND PASTORAL CARE

1. People were not made to go through hardships and sickness and heartaches alone

2. As caregivers and facilitators of wholeness, our objective should always be to make it possible for the sick, the suffering, the disabled, and the dying, to come to the knowledge that God cares and is intent on relieving them of their condition

3. If by our compassionate presence and prayers we are able to nurture the sick into recognizing God and claiming their own value in Him, forgiveness, healing, health, and even dying in hope, can become attainable goals

4. As pastoral caregivers, our task is to help people get in touch with God

5. The people we visit need to be seen as more than quotas that we quickly fill from our visitation lists

6. Depending on the physical condition of a patient, I do not believe that we should spend excessive amounts of time in the hospital room exhausting a patient with extensive conversations

7. Diversity is also critical to the pastoral care process because it makes us deeply aware that the spiritual, physical, emotional, mental, and medical conditions that so often impact human beings are not limited to any one gender, race, culture, or ethnicity

8. Whether or not we like it, or whether or not we are willing to accept it, our churches and health care facilities are increasingly becoming diverse places and institutions

9. My advice is for us not to go into ministry and or pastoral care situations with preconceived notions of what the situation is or what the outcome should be

10. To enhance our diverse ministries and pastoral care methodologies and approaches in diverse settings, we need to take time to develop some understanding of prevailing multicultural demands and practices in the contexts within which we serve

11. Let us look back at the areas we have already covered

—

PAUSE FOR REVIEW

SEE QUESTIONS BELOW TO HELP GUIDE YOUR DISCUSSIONS. YOU MAY ADD YOUR OWN QUESTIONS THAT MAY HAVE COME OUT OF YOUR STUDY EXPERIENCE TOGETHER

EVALUATION/DISCUSSION QUESTIONS

1. **Giving examples, talk for a moment about what you think the author means when he says that, "we are caregivers and facilitators of wholeness"**

2. **What is your understanding of the writer's use of the term "compassionate presence?"**

3. What are some ways that we may empower the sick and dying and families coping with sickness and death, to face death and sicknesses with hope?

4. Caring for human sickness takes precedence over race, religion, and gender. Discuss this statement based on the content of today's lessons and your personal experience

5. The author advices that we should not go into situations with preconceived notions of what the situation is or what the outcome should be. Discuss this in light of diversity, contextual situations and the effectiveness of pastoral care

CHAPTER SEVEN

LIVING ESCHATOLOGICALLY

THE IMPACT OF ESCHATOLOGY ON OUR SPIRITUAL FORMATION AND TRANSFORMATION

Devotional Exercise
Welcome/Greetings
Sharing of prayer concerns
Prayer
Hymn(s) of the day
Scripture selection(s) for today

Prayer:
Most holy and eternal God, as I/we wait for the return of Your beloved Son and my/our blessed Savior, Redeemer and Lord, I/we pray that You would give me/us patience in waiting. Renew in me/us the motivation to serve others and shine Your light in a darkened world. Let my/our waiting be an opportunity to develop perseverance, faith, obedience, and the desire to actively serve You. Mold me/us into the likeness of You Son and draw me/us into Your divine life so that I/we may be positioned and ready for your promised eternity. In the name of Jesus I/we pray, Amen!

Prayer:
Dear God, eternal and loving You are. You have taught us to love because You first loved us. Implant in us Your Spirit of love so that we may love You and others as You have loved us. Help us today to give a little more of ourselves to others through service, concern, and love for Your people wherever they may be and in whatever station in life, circumstances may place them. As You lifted us through Your Son Jesus Christ, empower us to lift up others so that they too may come to know the love we have found in Christ. As we go through this day with the mind to serve You by serving others, grant us grace. Prevent us from falling into the temptation to withdraw ourselves from service because of the hate and meanness around us. With Your love firmly fixed in our hearts, give us the boldness to enter every situation and life's challenges depending on the sufficiency of Your grace to get us through. Assure and sustain us wherever and whenever we may be despised and rejected. Give us, dear God eternal, the gift of gratitude and appreciation for those who embrace us in our efforts to make disciples for Christ. Hear and deliver us we pray and we will be careful to give You all of the glory and the praise. This we pray in the name of Jesus, Amen!

Scriptures: Ps 43:5; 98:9; Dan 7:13; 12:13; Mt 24:30; Mk 8:38; Lu 5:24; 12:37, 40; Jn 14:3, 8, 28; Acts 24:15; 1 Cor 2:9-12; Phil 3:20-21; Col 1:5; 3:1-4; 1 Th 4:16; Tit 2:13; Heb 6:18-19; 1 Pet 5:4; 1 Jn 3: 2; Rev 1:17; 7:9-17

Hymns:
"My Hope Is Built On Nothing Less"
"Blessed Assurance"
"Jesus Keep Me Near The Cross"
"The Strife Is O'er, The Battle Done"
"I Want To Be Ready"
"When We All Get To Heaven"
"O, Come, O Come, Emmanuel"
"Jesus, Joy Of Our Desiring"
"Soon And Very Soon"
"Lead On King Jesus"
"I'll Fly Away"
"Love So Amazing"
"Love Divine All Love Excelling"
"Love Lifted Me"

Objectives:
To help us:

- Understand the transforming effect of eschatology on the believer's behavior and attitude
- Understand how we live in the paradox of time and eternity (the now and the not yet of our Christian experience and hope)
- See how eschatology is active participation in the mission of God to transform the world
- Develop and understanding of how living in the present is both our preparation and at the same time, a foretaste of the not yet and future glory
- Understand how eschatology is a call to active living and service in community as opposed to a passive and individual search for piety
- Understand how eschatology is an alternative to a secular world view of time and eternity
- See how eschatological hope is an alternative to the failed optimism of world view

1. OVERVIEW

Two of the most anticipated events in Christendom are the Advent of Christ and His promised return. Every generation before and since Christ has lived and died in anticipation of His coming, and now His promised return. The anticipation of both events has motivated people to live a lifestyle that is in a constant state of readiness and perhaps for some, a state of uncertainty.

In this chapter, I will offer a critical analysis of eschatology and its impact on the believer's faith formation and spiritual transformation. My objective will be to show how the nearness of God which is wrapped up in our anticipation of the return of Jesus Christ, leads ultimately to the formation of attitudes and behaviors that are pleasing to God. How that formation and or behavioral adjustment lends itself to the believer's spiritual transformation and growth in Christ will preoccupy us at this level of our discussion.

While eschatological themes such as life after death and judgment may be referenced in our discussion of eschatology, it is not my intention to investigate or develop these eschatological themes. My objective, without being exhaustive, is to examine the implication of eschatology for Christian living today. In general terms, I will focus on how our spiritual transformation is impacted by the hope that is invoked by the eschatological promises of Scripture as they relate to the return of Jesus Christ and our glorious future with Him.

How the promised return of Christ stirs up the human response to devotion and commitment to God, and how that anticipation moves us by the aid of the Holy Spirit to engage ourselves in continuous worship and the demonstration of mercy and love toward our neighbors, in anticipation of the return of Christ, will be important to our examination and discussion. Also, how eschatology consistently challenges us to actively engage ourselves in the making of disciples for Christ, rather than conforming to passive waiting and individual pursuit of piety, will form critical components of our consideration. It should not be presumed however, that Christian deeds, whether by devotions to God or the extension of mercy and love to our neighbors, are coerced by any threat of judgment or hell as it relates to the end times. As believing people, we continue to worship God and work through mission and Christian witnessing in the "meanwhile," because we are motivated by love for God and our neighbor. How the liturgy of worship and mission finds continuous expression and purpose in our anticipation of the greater glory, and how that anticipation leads to the spiritual transformation of the Christian life will constitute our probing of eschatology. The intriguing implications of a realized eschatology and eschatology expected, as they relate to the paradox of time and eternity, will grab our attention. Also, how Jesus Christ and the hope that His resurrection instills makes Him an alternative to a world view of the human condition of hopelessness and despair, will form the overall backdrop of this chapter.

As noted above, eschatological hope should not cause us to become lost in our personal quest for an undetermined place beyond the here and now. Instead, such hope should keep us grounded in Jesus and become for us a continuous source of inspiration and joy for virtuous living in the present. Living eschatologically should therefore be taken to mean living joyfully in the present based on the glorious blessings and grace of God already experienced, and faithfully serving God and participating in the mission of Christ, in anticipation of His return. Such anticipation and active engagements also give opportunity to the Holy Spirit who is all the time seeking to cultivate our spiritual formation as He works to spiritually transform, empower us to serve, keep our hope alive, bring forth the fruit of His Spirit in us, and position us for eternity.

2. WHAT IS ESCHATOLOGY?

1. Knight defines eschatology as the "language of promise which offers a future to those who respond to God's grace with faith"

2. With our focus shifted from talk about a future promise to real expectations concerning the Object of the promise, and even though eschatology is an expectation that is oriented toward the future, the very implications of eschatology instill within us the urgent desire to become engaged in the continuous activity of Christ in the present time

3. Eschatology as a lifestyle is founded on three premises

4. It is my position that even though eschatology relates to a promise which offers a future to those who respond to God with faith, this is not a future that is separated from the present

5. Because our present time with Christ is not divorced from our future with Him, to keep our heads stuck in a future heaven without any earthly grounding would be to neutralize the very purpose of eschatology

6. In the content of this book, eschatology is not viewed as the expectation of gloom and doom, destruction and condemnation, and a coming judgment with apocalyptic and Armageddon proportions that are so often projected to mark the end of time as we know it

7. Eschatology literally fills us with existential hope by giving us something glorious to look forward to

8. Certainly, our belief in and anticipation of the second coming of Christ should not disable us from performing active service

9. I believe that the content of eschatology ought to be existentially taught, believed, and lived in every moment of our earthly lives

10. Consequently, in the content of this book, eschatology is viewed and presented as a moral model that inspires Christian believers to aspire through grace to live holy before God in every living age

———

PAUSE FOR
QUESTIONS/COMMENTS/CLARIFICATIONS

EVALUATION/DISCUSSION QUESTIONS

1. **What is your understanding of the term eschatology?**

2. **Based on the definition and overview of eschatology presented at this point of the study, what new idea or information do you take away from the study?**

3. **"Eschatology is hope that is sustained by and in the Holy Spirit." Explain this statement with the help of scripture.**

4. **Please take a moment to share with us your hope and expectations for eternity**

3. ESCHATOLOGY AS A COMPONENT OF SPIRITUAL FORMATION/TRANSFORMATION (SECTION ONE)

1. Eschatology is an essential component of spiritual transformation by virtue of the futuristic expectations concerning the return of Christ and eternity with God that such expectations invoke

2. As we were created in the image of God, thus expressing the divine intent and the possibility of human communion with God, eschatologically, the likeness of God is a moral likeness into which God intends His redeemed sons and daughters to grow

3. Implied by spiritual transformation in a narrow sense, then, is a process of renewal in the Christian attitude and behavior that are being directed by the Holy Spirit toward God's eternity

4. This hope in Christ, who promised to return, continues to be a source of nurture and spiritual formation for us

5. At this stage of our becoming or being transformed to be more like Jesus, a set of new variables take over our outlook on life and eternity

6. Eschatological expectations reshape the believer's life

—

| PAUSE FOR REVIEW |

SEE QUESTIONS BELOW TO HELP GUIDE YOUR DISCUSSIONS. YOU MAY ADD YOUR OWN QUESTIONS THAT MAY HAVE COME OUT OF YOUR STUDY EXPERIENCE TOGETHER

EVALUATION/DISCUSSION QUESTIONS

1. **How has this lesson helped your understanding of what it means to live eschatological lives?**

2. **In what ways do you think that eschatology is a source of spiritual transformation?**

3. **How do you think your life may be changed from this new awareness?**

ESCHATOLOGY AS A COMPONENT OF SPIRITUAL FORMATION/TRANSFORMATION (SECTION TWO)

1. Eschatology as an important component of spiritual transformation engages the Father, Son, and Holy Spirit in the formation or reshaping of the Christian's life

2. If indeed, eschatology is a theology of hope, this theology of hope is a theology of transformation

3. As we submit to the sanctifying power of the Holy Spirit, then, our re-education and or the reorientation of our minds toward God that began to germinate in worship, developed in mission, now reaches its final trimester of expectancy

4. Not only that, He who has ascended to the right hand of God the Father, continues to be our advocate before God, while making intercessions for us

5. The ultimate revelation of the glory of Christ and our transformation into that glory is attested to by the First Epistle of John

6. Eschatology is spiritually transforming because the promise that eschatology proclaims, and the expectations that it instills in us, change the way we think and act

7. We are transformed by the renewing of our minds to prove or live according to the acceptable and perfect will of God[26]

.

—

PAUSE FOR REVIEW
SEE QUESTIONS BELOW TO HELP GUIDE YOUR DISCUSSIONS. YOU MAY ADD YOUR OWN QUESTIONS THAT MAY HAVE COME OUT OF YOUR STUDY EXPERIENCE TOGETHER

EVALUATION/DISCUSSION QUESTIONS

1. **What do you think it means for a person's life to be spiritually reshaped?**

---

[26] Rom 12:2

2. According to the author, "If indeed eschatology is a theology of hope, this theology of hope is a theology of transformation." Examine and discuss this statement based on your understanding of the theology of hope, the promises of the Lord Jesus and the effects of eschatology on our spiritual lives

3. Why do you think it is necessary to submit to the sanctifying power of the Holy Spirit in order for our re-education concerning God to begin?

4. What impact has this lesson made on your understanding of what it means to live eschatological lives?

5. How has today's lesson impacted your faith and view of Christian practice and hope?

4. ESCHATOLOGICAL LIVING: MAKING OURSELVES ACCESSIBLE THROUGH ACTIVE WITNESSING

1. While there may not be much talk about eschatology as a serious stand of theology in contemporary churches and theological discussions, though perhaps somewhat dormant, there is within the Church and society a sort of renewed interest in the return of Christ

2. As God made Himself accessible to us through Christ and daily available to us through the presence of the Holy Spirit, we are called to make ourselves accessible to those to whom we are called to witness

3. As we wait expectantly for Christ, eschatological hope is therefore grounded in the accessible grace of God that reaches out

4. Full salvation is not a static experience gained in isolation. Salvation is an active experience that is grounded in faith in the accessible life, ministry, and finished work of Christ

5. Eschatology does not call us to live passive lifestyles locked away as it were, in our individual cocoons

6. The notion of active engagement in Christian service as opposed to a passive escapist mindset resonates well with the message of Christ who tells us to work while it is day for the night comes when we cannot see to work

7. To that extent, eschatology forces us out of our everyday fixation on ourselves and renders unacceptable, any desire to withdraw into isolation in search of personal piety

8. The nearness of God, then, is salvation for those who not only take notice but also act upon that awareness with faith and proceed to participate in His work of calling the world to Him

—

PAUSE FOR REVIEW
SEE QUESTIONS BELOW TO HELP GUIDE YOUR DISCUSSIONS. YOU MAY ADD YOUR OWN QUESTIONS THAT MAY HAVE COME OUT OF YOUR STUDY EXPERIENCE TOGETHER

EVALUATION/DISCUSSION QUESTIONS

1. **What are your thoughts about seeking personal holiness through isolation?**

2. **Make a list outlining the differences between active participation in Christian mission and a passive mindset**

3. **How can the Christian life become an expression of God's descending love and out reaching grace in the world?**

4. What do you suggest as the best course of actions for Christians to pursue as they wait for the return of Christ?

5. What do you think accessible grace is and how do you explain that in terms of God's actions toward us?

5. ESCHATOLOGY REALIZED, ESCHATOLOGY EXPECTED (THE PARADOX OF TIME AND ETERNITY) (SECTION ONE)

1. According to Konig, "Eschatology is not restricted to a future expectation…."[27]

2. The notion of realized eschatology finds reasonable support in the New Testament, in the Gospel of John in particular

3. This undoubtedly speaks of God's gift of eschatological salvation

4. Eschatology as a lifestyle is therefore a present living experience of Christ, as well as our living in a hope that transcends time and space whereby the Christ we experience now, is the Christ we yet hope for

—

---

[27] A. Konig, <u>The Eclipse of Christ in Eschatology,</u> (Grand Rapids, MI: Erdmans, 1989), 15

EVALUATION/DISCUSSION QUESTIONS

1. **If eschatology is the language of promise and something expected in the future, what do we mean by realized eschatology? You may use Bible verses that you recall to help with your response**

2. **"Indeed, the kingdom and reign of God has come in the person of Christ and has penetrated and taken up residence in believers' lives and hearts." What do you understand by this statement?**

3. **Share with us how you think eschatology may be considered a lifestyle?**

ESCHATOLOGY REALIZED, ESCHATOLOGY EXPECTED (THE PARADOX OF TIME AND ETERNITY) (SECTION TWO)

1. Realistically, the promise is being experienced now.

2. It is certainly conceivable that in order to realize God's glorious future, it must be recognized and lived in the present so that it may be diligently and faithfully pursued and attained to as grace moves us from glory to glory[28]

3. Having already received the gift of salvation in the present, we have a constant yearning for a future glory and communion with God

4. Such is the paradox of Christian life and living

---

[28] See chapter two, section F "Moving From Glory To Glory"

5. As surely as Christ came and called our attention to the kingdom of God which is at hand, or, indeed, already here, the eschatological reign of Christ has already begun in the reign and dispensation of grace

6. Consequently, the power to live in Christ and the manifestations of the fruits of the kingdom are available now because our past, present, and future, are inextricably wrapped up in God who is the same yesterday, today, and forever

7. Assuredly, the promises of God are as sure as the realization of the promises

8. Indeed, the kingdom and reign of God has come in the person of Christ, is dwelling among us, and has already taken authority of believers' lives and hearts

———

PAUSE FOR REVIEW

SEE QUESTIONS BELOW TO HELP GUIDE YOUR DISCUSSIONS. YOU MAY ADD YOUR OWN QUESTIONS THAT MAY HAVE COME OUT OF YOUR STUDY EXPERIENCE TOGETHER

EVALUATION/DISCUSSION QUESTION

1. **How would you explain the notion that we are already living as kingdom citizens?**

2. **According to the writer, "Realistically, the promise is being experienced now because the God of the promise is with us." From the point of view of the presence and operation of God in our lives in the present time, in what ways would you say that the promise of eternity is being realized now?**

3. **What do you think the writer intends when he says, "Such is the paradox of Christian life and living"**

Eschatology Realized, Eschatology Expected (The Paradox Of Time And Eternity) (Section Three)

1. Living the life of eternity or living eschatologically must therefore be taken to mean living joyfully in the present, as we are inspired by a promised future that is guaranteed

2. When we speak then, of the dawning of the kingdom of God as Jesus announced at the beginning of His ministry, we can conclude that God's present reign implies a realized eschatology

3. The Christian life is indeed "a process toward an eschatological goal attainable in its fullness in the world to come, but attainable in part within time and history"[29]

4. Salvation is indeed a continuous process

—

PAUSE FOR REVIEW

SEE QUESTIONS BELOW TO HELP GUIDE YOUR DISCUSSIONS. YOU MAY ADD YOUR OWN QUESTIONS THAT MAY HAVE COME OUT OF YOUR STUDY EXPERIENCE TOGETHER

Evaluation/Discussion Questions

1. **Jesus came saying the kingdom of God is (here) at hand." In what sense do you think the kingdom reign of God has already begun?**

2. **God has promised never to leave us alone. How has this promise made the difference in your personal faith journey?**

---

[29] Clarence L. Bence, "Processive Eschatology: A Wesleyan Alternative," <u>Wesleyan Theological Journal</u> 14-15, (1979), (45-59), 54

3. **What is prevenient grace and what do you think are some benefits of prevenient grace?**

6. ESCHATOLOGY AND COMMUNITY: OUR CONTINUOUS WORKING FOR CHRIST IN THE WORLD

1. Eschatology as hope is a source of inspiration for the Christian's continuous work and participation in the ministry of Christ

2. We are called, changed, and inspired to do the work of Christ in the world

3. Certainly, righteousness is not grounded in works; but good works are the manifestations of our having been made righteous

4. In James 2:26 for example, the author indicates that "faith without works is dead"

5. To effectively serve God and witness to the saving power of Jesus in the world, individual pursuits must give way to the uplifting of community

6. Active witnessing implies the proclamation of the love of God and the Good News of salvation in Christ

7. Hope that is not proclaimed in the community, but is reserved for selfish, passive, individual pursuits and denominational monopoly, does not spring from Christian eschatology

—

PAUSE FOR LESSON REVIEW
QUESTIONS/COMMENTS/CLARIFICATIONS
BREAK INTO GROUP DISCUSSIONS

EVALUATION/DISCUSSION QUESTIONS

1. How would you say that eschatology inspires Christian service in the world?

2. Share with us your understanding of the "continuous work and ministry of Christ"

3. What is meant by working in community and why is the concept and practice of community service important for Christian ministry?

4. Why do you think it is necessary for us to deny ourselves when it comes to Christian service?

5. "Faith without works is dead." What is your opinion? In what ways can faith be considered dead and how can faith become alive and active?

6. What does the author mean by the statement, "To effectively serve God and witness to the saving power of Jesus in the world, individual pursuits must give way to the uplifting of community?"

7. Do you think you are an active witness for Christ in the world? If not, how can we help to encourage your desire to witness for Christ?

7. ESCHATOLOGICAL HOPE AS AN ALTERNATIVE TO A SECULAR WORLDVIEW AND FAULTY HUMAN OPTIMISM THE ESCHATOLOGICAL TASK OF THE CHURCH (SECTION ONE)

1. Eschatology is where the road forks

2. As we are caught up, as it were, between time and eternity, the task of the Church is to shift the world's view from physical, temporary optimism, human systems and day-to-day pursuits of mundane, hopeless and purposeless things, to matters of hope and eternal value

3. Eternity helps us make sense of time

4. Not walking as the rest of the world walks should not be taken as judgmental or separatist in its emphasis

5. Whoever you are and wherever you are, alone, in Sunday school, Bible study or small group study, alone at home, in the park or in prison, you are not reading or studying this book and this section of it by chance

6. All you need to do in response to what Christ has already done is truly confess Him as the Son of the living God, truly believe that He died for you, sincerely surrender to Him and accept Him as your Lord and Savior, and you shall be saved to the glory of God[30]

——

PAUSE FOR LESSON REVIEW
QUESTIONS/COMMENTS/CLARIFICATIONS
BREAK INTO GROUP DISCUSSIONS

EVALUATION/DISCUSSION QUESTIONS

1. **"Eschatology is where the road forks." Explain this statement in terms of end time choices and Christian discipleship**

2. **What are some of the reasons or conviction that you have for projecting Jesus as the alternative to secular world view and the correct way to God?**

---

[30] Jn 5:24; Rom 10:9; 1 Jn 1:9

3. What do we do in response to what Christ has done on the cross?

Eschatological Hope: An Alternative To A Secular Worldview And Faulty Human Optimism
The Eschatological Task Of The Church
(Section Two)

1. By secular world standards, human knowledge, philosophical systems, and self-help programs and seminars seem capable of offering at least some semblance of optimism though transitory in nature

2. Lasting hope can only be found in God's activity and presence in the world[31]

3. Hope is only found in God and will only be truly realized in Him and His eschatological Christ

4. As believing servants of God, having known the severity, oppressive, and destructive nature of sin, our task is to be witness bearers of God's forgiveness in the world

5. Our eschatological task is to take the Gospel message of salvation to the world

6. I give you not a philosophy. I offer you not a culture and certainly not a business. All I offer you is Jesus Christ, the way, the truth, and the life

7. You may say that I am arrogant to affirm this conviction and for projecting Jesus as the correct way to God when there are so many religions and faith positions in the world. Let me illustrate this conviction

---

[31] Ps 146:3-7; Is. 30:1, 31:3; Jer. 17:5-8

8. Now then, let me ask you, if you saw a valued friend in error, would you just sit there and say nothing because you do not want to offend or embarrass your friend?

9. The world, often through the guise of other faith positions, has become good at imitating the light,[32] but the world does not have the power to be that Light or the capacity to duplicate that Light

10. For me, at a personal level, believing in and experiencing Jesus Christ in my life has been the source of my greatest assurance and comfort

---

PAUSE FOR LESSON REVIEW
QUESTIONS/COMMENTS/CLARIFICATIONS
BREAK INTO GROUP DISCUSSIONS

EVALUATION/DISCUSSION QUESTIONS

1. **Where do you draw the line between a secular world system, built around human philosophies, self-help programs, and fleeting optimism and the promises of God based on scripture?**

2. **Given the existence of many religions, do you think it is wrong or arrogant to offer guidance or direction to someone going in the "wrong direction" based on your faith position?**

3. **Please share with us how knowing or having a personal relationship with Jesus has impacted your life**

8. RATIONALES FOR PROJECTING CHRIST AS THE ONLY ALTERNATIVE AND HOPE (AN OVERVIEW)

Hope in Christ is God's divine alternative for a world lost in hopelessness and despair. God has equipped the Christian community with the necessary means to offer Christ as an alternative to human despair and hopelessness on several

---

[32] 2 Cor 11:14-15

grounds. These are: (i) The evidence of creation, faith and the pervasiveness of God's grace and activity in the world; (ii) The resurrection of Jesus; (iii) The promised return of Jesus Christ; (iv) God cannot lie (The Immutability of God); and (v) History is not accidental (God Controls Time and History). Let us take a moment to examine these reasons for our projection of Christ in our witness to the world.

(i) The Evidence of Creation, Faith, and the Activities of God in The World

1. Our first alternative and response to a secular worldview is the pervasiveness of God's grace, presence, and activity in the world

2. If it is indeed in God that we live, move and have our being, and if knowledge of God and faith in Christ is eternal life,[33] it follows that God's overarching providence guides human affairs and the entire cosmos, to their completion in Him

3. Faith in God makes the difference between our grasping for the straws of human optimism with the intention of not drowning in the miseries of life, and our holding firmly and staying grounded on a belief in the assurance of God's promise

4. Blind faith is the human term for human pursuits that are not based on any prior examination and knowledge of what we are getting ourselves into or without knowing what the outcomes are likely to be

5. The Apostle Paul speaks of the things we are gifted to see as "a mystery, the hidden wisdom"[34] that is concealed from the world, but made known to those who have taken notice of God's nearness, and believe in His Christ

6. This eschatological and rather spiritual grasp of a reality beyond the tangible world, is intended to equip us to live in hope while confidently offering the world this hope in God

---

[33] Jn 17:3
[34] See 1 Cor 2:7

7. Christian faith is not without basis or evidence or substance

8. The evidence of creation and the evidence of the resurrection of Jesus are supporting pillars of our faith

9. I submit that the human opposition to the principles and Object of faith, God, is one of convenience and a cop-out for easing the human conscience

10. While human ideologies and systems may offer some degree of optimism, that optimism at best, is rather fleeting and therefore unfulfilling

11. The human heart is persistently searching for fulfillment and satisfaction because human systems, philosophies, and scientific discoveries still leave a void in us that only our encounter with God can fill

12. Contrary to popular secular opinions, faith in God is not the Christian's safety net

—

PAUSE FOR REVIEW

SEE QUESTIONS BELOW TO HELP GUIDE YOUR DISCUSSIONS. YOU MAY ADD YOUR OWN QUESTIONS THAT MAY HAVE COME OUT OF YOUR STUDY EXPERIENCE TOGETHER

EVALUATION/DISCUSSION QUESTIONS

1. **How would you explain the term "the pervasiveness of God's grace?"**

2. **Share with us how you faith keeps you grounded in a world so filled with confusion and uncertainty**

3. **How would you explain that the Christian's faith is not blind faith? You may use scripture to support you response**

4. **The writer says, "...The human opposition to the principles and Object of faith, God, is one of convenience and a cop-out for easing the human conscience." How would you explain this statement?**

5. **Why do you think the human heart and desire are unfulfilled without our connection to God?**

(ii) The Resurrection of Jesus
(Section One)

1. Our second alternative to the prevailing secular worldview on the matter of life, death, and the meaning of life beyond the grave, is the Christian claim and evidence of the resurrection of Jesus

2. The resurrection of Jesus is a good indication that when you live your life believing God and trusting His providence, when you are abused and mistreated, even in death, He will vindicate you and take your life to greater levels

3. When you know, despite the negativity, the defeats, and the hopelessness around you, that you can have victory in the present time and hope for a better future, life and eternity become something to care about

4. If the resurrection is true, and we believe that it is, in a world filled with skeptics, many need to rethink their positions, reorder their lives, and make the changes that faith demands so that they too can become children of the resurrection

5. The New Testament has nowhere described the actual raising of Jesus from the grave

6. In retrospect, Jesus did predict victory beyond the grave for Himself and His divine purpose

The Resurrection of Jesus
(Section Two)

1. Do you still have doubts about the resurrection of Jesus?

2. Using five other supporting sources of evidence, let us further examine the resurrection of Jesus

3. Calvary seemed to have been an irreversible disaster and a hopeless ending

4. The resurrection, a fable, an illusion? I do not think so!

5. Also, by the resurrection of Christ and His subsequent appearances to the disciples, their fears were removed, their faith received assurance, and their ministry received power

6. The resurrection demonstrates once and for all, that it is God, not any human that is in control of life, time, and eternity

7. The dignity of God implanted in us is of eternal value my friend. The resurrection of Jesus affirmed that value

8. The resurrection affirms that death is not the end or the master of the believer's destiny

9. By the resurrection of Christ, a believing humanity is given a vision of life that does not end at death, but begins anew in a more glorious form of existence

10. In God, humanity has a future that goes beyond the fatalistic and meaningless ethos of the world

11. An empty tomb without the living Christ would have left the matter still open to debate and uncertainty

12. Based on the resurrection of Jesus, Christian eschatology, through the active witness of the Christian Community, needs to be an ongoing challenge to the dominant ethos of the secular world where hopelessness, despair, and death have been projected to have the last laugh

—

PAUSE FOR REVIEW
SEE QUESTIONS BELOW TO HELP GUIDE YOUR DISCUSSIONS. YOU MAY ADD YOUR OWN QUESTIONS THAT MAY HAVE COME OUT OF YOUR STUDY EXPERIENCE TOGETHER

EVALUATION/DISCUSSION QUESTIONS

1. **"Jesus lives!" Explain this statement using the witness of the New Testament and other writers concerning the resurrection of Jesus**

2. **In what ways is the resurrection of Jesus a source of life and hope for the Christian faith and witness?**

3. **How is the resurrection of Jesus a reversal of the hopelessness and despair that came from the events of Good Friday?**

(iii) The Promised Return of Jesus Christ

1. The third reason for our continuous witness to the world and our projection of Jesus as hope for the human despair is based fundamentally on our convictions regarding the promised return of Jesus, as attested to by Scripture.[35]

---

[35] Ps 98:9; Mt 26:64; Mk 14:62; Lk 21:27-28; Acts 1:11; Heb 9:28; 2 Pet 3:10,13

2. Based on the promised return of Jesus, as an eschatological community waiting for His return, we need to be diligent about our proclamation of that promise

3. Because of the promise and because of the integrity of the One who promised, the risen and exalted Christ, this eschatological expectation warrants us to active proclamation of the promise even at the expense of our own comfort and convenience

4. Having sensed the calling of God on your life for active and participative witness in the world, are you willing to suffer inconveniences so that Christ may be preached and so that people may come to know the power of God?

5. Because of the promised return of Christ, we are persuaded that in Christ, the regenerated life has become a life of glorious hope

(iv) God cannot lie
(The Immutability of God)

1. The fourth basis on which to build our witness to the world is our conviction that God cannot lie

2. We have hope of eternal life because the God who cannot lie has promised it

3. God cannot lie; and by virtue of His immutability, He will not change His mind or go back on His word

4. If God changes, He would not qualify to deal with the changes we go through and have to deal with in time and history

(v) History Is Not Accidental
(God Controls Time and History)

1. The fifth premise upon which our proclamation of a hopeful outcome for humanity is built is the premise that history is not accidental

2. Human history, time and space, as we know them, find their completion in God because He is the Author and Finisher of time and space

3. Because of the variableness or changing nature of time and history, without a constant and sovereign power to guide it, total and reckless abandon would ensue

4. The God that we glorify is of infinite duration who sits enthroned as sovereign King forever[36]

5. Everything has its beginning and ending in God

6. Some may say that God does not control history because history is something that has already happened

7. As the providential and sovereign God, nothing escapes the Great CEO of heaven and earth

8. And so you may ask, "How do we reconcile God's existence and sovereignty with human suffering in time and history?"

---

[36] Ps 29:10

9. I am sure you believe in the existence of attributes such as courage, generosity, beneficence, justice, forgiveness, mercy, even truth

10. In the midst of evil and human suffering, I do know that God gives grace for those times when our spirit is hurting and we are driven to the breaking point

11. When evil overwhelms us and when trials come, it helps to see them in relation to God's will

12. When I am in hardship and when I experience suffering, and the occasions have been many, they have never been occasions or opportunities for me to turn away from God

13. Our confidence as an eschatological community soars because the Holy Spirit has lavished our hearts and minds and faith with the truth of God's word and evidence of God's love for all of us demonstrated through Christ

14. By virtue of the present operation of the Holy Spirit in our lives and community, we are equipped to remain firm in our purpose and diligent in our witness to the world despite the changing circumstances around us

15. As we continue to witness to the power of God in the world, notwithstanding the opposition we may face, and despite our human sufferings and frailties, we should not fear what mankind can do[37]

16. The one power, the one presence, the one constant, the one great order of the universe, is God

———

---

[37] Heb 13:6; See also Ps 27, 46: 2, 49:5, 91:5, 118:6; Lk 1:74; 2 Tim 1:7; 1 Jn 4:18

| PAUSE FOR REVIEW |

SEE QUESTIONS BELOW TO HELP GUIDE YOUR DISCUSSIONS. YOU MAY
ADD YOUR OWN QUESTIONS THAT MAY HAVE COME OUT OF YOUR STUDY
EXPERIENCE TOGETHER

EVALUATION/DISCUSSION QUESTIONS

1. **How is the hope that Jesus offers different from human optimism?**

2. **If you were to share with someone, who is probably hopeless, about belief in God in order to develop hope, which of the five methods above would you use to help you do so?**

3. **History is not accidental. God controls time and history. How would you explain these statements in light of prevailing human suffering and the existence of a loving and compassionate God?**

4. **In what ways has this lesson benefited you?**

9. WHAT DO WE DO WHILE WE WAIT?

1. As we wait for the return of Christ, it is imperative that we continue to worship and practice discipleship

2. The very belief in Christ's returning necessitates us working to sustain the change in the new order that He has already established

3. If indeed we believe that something is wrong with the world around us, as the redeemed of God, we should also believe that we have been mandated to fix it

4. It was in the world that God sent His only begotten Son to redeem it[38]

5. Our redemption comes with the responsibility of seeking out others as we engage ourselves in Christ's ongoing ministry of reconciliation

6. If our purpose in the world is to make Christ known, then the methodology for doing so needs to be our out-reaching love and service

7. As we prayerfully wait for the return of Christ, let us dedicate ourselves to living out the meaning of hope through active service and witness in the world

—

PAUSE FOR REVIEW
SEE QUESTIONS BELOW TO HELP GUIDE YOUR DISCUSSIONS. YOU MAY ADD YOUR OWN QUESTIONS THAT MAY HAVE COME OUT OF YOUR STUDY EXPERIENCE TOGETHER

EVALUATION/DISCUSSION QUESTIONS

1. **In your opinion, what are some of the ways that the promised return of Christ becomes a matter of urgency for worship and Christian service to the world?**

2. **Making disciples for Christ by the authority of the word of God demands that we preach as well as live that word in the world. Using your understanding of faith and the practice of faith, explain this statement**

3. **"Our redemption comes with a responsibility..." In your own words, explain this statement**

---

[38] Mk 16:15; Jn 15:16; Acts 1:8; Col 1:6

CHAPTER EIGHT

MOTIVATED AND TRANSFORMED BY LOVE

Devotional Exercise
Welcome/Greetings
Sharing of prayer concerns
Prayer
Hymn(s) of the day
Scripture selection(s) for today

Prayer:
Dearest and most loving God, we give You thanks for the great love that You have given us through our Lord Jesus. We confess that we have not loved You with our whole heart. We have failed to love our neighbors and we have been slow in responding to the cry of the needy. Forgive us we pray and renew in us Your Spirit of love so that by Your indwelling Spirit, we may be moved to respond to You and others with love. Move us to joyful obedience we pray. As we set out to serve others today, inspire us by Your Holy Spirit to do so with an attitude of love. This we pray in the wonderful name of Jesus, Amen!

Hymns:
"Come, Thou Fount Of Every Blessing"
"I Love To Tell The Story"
"My God, I Love Thee"
"Take My Life And Let It Be"
"O How I Love Jesus"
"And Can It Be That I Should Gain?"
"Jesus Loves Me"

Scriptures: Lev 19:18; Ps 91:14; Prov 10:12; Mic 6:8; Mt 5:44-46; Jn 14:15, 15:12-17; 1 2; 1 Cor 13; Cor 5:14a; Rom 12:9, 13:8; Gal 5:6-15; 1 Tim 1:5, 4:12; Heb 13:1-2; 1 Jn 4:7-21(also 1 Jn. chapters 3, 4, and 5)

Objectives:
To help us:

- Understand love as the divine economy of God

- Value the importance of loving God and neighbor
- See the demonstration of love as an indication of our having been changed

1. LOVE AS THE DIVINE ECONOMY OF GOD

1. Love is the divine economy of God that permeates everything that God does for us

2. Love as a divine economy or method is the impetus that God uses to manage and disperse His favor toward us

3. God's sustained presence and self-revelation through His creative, redemptive, and sanctifying work are the results of God's overflowing love for us

4. In creation, God began His mission of love toward us

5. Love is therefore the telos, the goal, the end result, the completion, and the fulfillment of all that God is and all that He does to us and for us

2. OUR RESPONSE TO THE LOVE OF GOD

1. Our response to God should always be one of love

2. As we continue to worship God, our worship response should always be one of self-giving love

3. Our loving response to the love that God has already given to us should never be based on our desire to get more from God

4. Everything that we are and hope to become is based on the knowledge that God loves us

5. The centrality of love in the Christian's scheme of things is critical for our understanding of all that we do in response to God

3. PRACTICING LOVE FOR GOD AND NEIGHBOR

1. Love for God and neighbor is a gift of grace

2. To love God and not love our neighbor makes us half a Christian

3. Love fulfills three functions in the Christian's life

4. As beneficiaries of divine grace, administered to us through the love of God in Christ Jesus, we do have a moral and ethical obligation to God and to each other

4. LOVE AS THE EVIDENCE THAT WE HAVE BEEN CHANGED

1. When the life that we live becomes a manifestation of love in the world, it also becomes demonstrative evidence that we have been changed

2. The love of God in us must therefore be manifested in deeds of kindness wrapped up in a life-style that reflects the abiding presence and perfect love of God

PAUSE FOR REVIEW

SEE QUESTIONS BELOW TO HELP GUIDE YOUR DISCUSSIONS. YOU MAY
ADD YOUR OWN QUESTIONS THAT MAY HAVE COME OUT OF YOUR STUDY
EXPERIENCE TOGETHER

EVALUATION/DISCUSSION QUESTIONS

1. "Love is the divine economy of God." Discuss this statement using your understanding of God's plan for our redemption and the dispensation of His gifts

2. In what ways do you think that God's mission of love began in creation?

3. List some ways that you think our self-giving love for God is inspired by as well as a mirroring of God's own Self-giving love

4. "To love God and not love our neighbor would be, according to Wesley, to settle for being half a Christian." Do you agree? Please give examples to support your position

5. List and discuss the three functions that love fulfills in the Christian's life

6. In what ways do you thing that we have both moral and ethical obligations to God and neighbor? Give examples and use illustrations to support your point of view

7. Do you agree that the demonstration of love for others is a good indicator of the extent to which we have been changed to be like Jesus?

CHAPTER NINE

ONE FINAL QUESTION: DO YOU KNOW JESUS?

Devotional Exercise
> Welcome/Greetings
> Sharing of prayer concerns
> Prayer
> Hymn(s) of the day
> Scripture selection(s) for today

Prayer:
God of wisdom and power, You gave us Your Son Jesus Christ because of Your great love for us. Open our eyes to the reality of Christ so that we may come to know, confess, and by faith in Your amazing grace, accept Him as Lord and Savior to the glory of Your name. We pray that You grant us a deeper knowledge of Jesus and fill our hearts with love that we may obtain the freedom and the joy to proclaim Christ in the world so that others can come to know Him and be saved. This we pray in the redeeming name of Jesus, Amen!

Selected Scriptures: Jn 8:19; Phil 3:10; 2 Tim 1:12, 2:25; 1 John 2:3-4

Hymns:
> "Jesus, Savior, Pilot Me"
> "Jesus Is All The World To Me"
> "I Know Whom I Have Believed"
> "Rejoice, The Lord Is King"
> "To God Be The Glory"
> "Hallelujah! What A Savior"
> "At The Name Of Jesus"
> "His Name Is Wonderful"
> "Hope Of The World"
> "Who Is He In Yonder Stall"

Objectives:
To help us:

- Develop some clarity about the person and work of the Lord Jesus
- Understand the importance of our faith confession in the process of salvation
- Understand the value of a personal relationship with Jesus
- Understand Jesus as the Way to God and our eternity with Him
- Understand the significance and benefits of the ascension of Jesus

1. ON KNOWING JESUS (SECTION ONE)

1. At a critical point in the life and ministry of Jesus, He was moved by the need to examine His disciples concerning their knowledge and understanding of Him

2. What we have here is a very important juncture in the teaching ministry of Jesus and a turning point in the life and faith development of the disciples

3. Jesus affirmed the absolute spiritual correctness of Peter's confession when He said in Matthew 16:17: "Blessed are you Simon Bar-Jonah, for flesh and blood has not revealed that to you, but My Father who is in heaven"

4. "Who do people say that I am?"

5. Many religious groups have different views as they relate to the person and nature of Christ

6. Jesus is more than the sum adulation of these religious points of view

7. The grave is empty because Jesus got up

8. As Jesus examined His disciples with that one-question final examination, He also examines each of us today— "Who do you say that I am?"

9. Do you know Jesus whom heaven and earth adore?

—

PAUSE FOR REVIEW
QUESTIONS/COMMENTS/CLARIFICATIONS
BREAK INTO GROUP DISCUSSIONS

ON KNOWING JESUS
(SECTION TWO)

1. Do you know who Jesus is?

2. Do you know Him as Savior and Lord or do you just think highly of Him?

3. Do you know Jesus, the Shepherd of your soul?

4. There is a difference between merely hearing about Jesus, reading about Jesus, reciting written works about Jesus, talking about Jesus, knowing of Jesus, and having a personal relationship with Jesus

—

PAUSE FOR REVIEW
SEE QUESTIONS BELOW TO HELP GUIDE YOUR DISCUSSIONS. YOU MAY
ADD YOUR OWN QUESTIONS THAT MAY HAVE COME OUT OF YOUR STUDY
EXPERIENCE TOGETHER

Evaluation/Discussion Questions

1. What do you think is the difference between reading about or hearing stories about Jesus and having a personal relationship with Him?

2. What do you think it means to have a personal relationship with Jesus?

3. Please share with us your own faith journey and relationship with Jesus. To what do you credit your personal growth in Christ?

4. John Tom, a young man from your neighborhood has never gone to church and has not come to know Jesus Christ as Lord and Savior. Write a letter to John Tom telling him about Jesus and the difference Jesus can make in his life

5. "The world will not go to hell because it does not have a Savior, but because it refuses to accept and believe the Savior, Jesus Christ." Discuss this statement in light of the existence of heaven and hell as well as the human will to choose

2. Our Necessary Confession Of Jesus

1. Your salvation from sin requires that you confess and believe in Jesus Christ

2. Our confession of Christ does two things at two distinct levels, at a personal level and at a relational level

3. Our confession of Christ, whether done privately or publicly, is essential for the foundation and development of the Christian's faith, Church, and Christian lifestyle

4. Knowing Jesus is God's gift of salvation to us. To receive the gift of salvation is to confess and believe in the bearer of that gift, Jesus Christ

5. Now that you have confessed and accepted Jesus Christ as your Lord and Savior, trust in Him and let Him lead you in order that you may discover the ways of God and begin to live a life that is pleasing to God

6. Having confessed Jesus Christ, and as you give your life and soul to Him, you can begin to live a life of victory

7. To have Jesus in your corner means that you have a lasting and eternal friend

8. Every soul shall be pinned against the wall of eternity and be required to answer this one question, "Who do you say that I am?"

—

PAUSE FOR REVIEW

SEE QUESTIONS BELOW TO HELP GUIDE YOUR DISCUSSIONS. YOU MAY ADD YOUR OWN QUESTIONS THAT MAY HAVE COME OUT OF YOUR STUDY EXPERIENCE TOGETHER

EVALUATION/DISCUSSION QUESTIONS

1. **Based on scripture, what is a confession?**

2. **Why do you think our confession of Christ is necessary for salvation? Please use scripture references to illustrate and support your response**

3. **In what ways do believing and knowing Jesus empower us to overcome our fears?**

4. **Share with us your personal experience of what Jesus means to your life**

3. JESUS, THE ONLY WAY

1. In the Gospel of John, Jesus declares Himself to be the Way, the Truth and the Life[39]

2. The Paths carved out by human constructs, customs, and traditions that are not expressly inspired and facilitated by the Spirit of God, are essentially carved out by human efforts and designs, and intended for self-fulfillment and sentimental self-gratification

———

| PAUSE FOR REVIEW |
| SEE QUESTIONS BELOW TO HELP GUIDE YOUR DISCUSSIONS. YOU MAY |
| ADD YOUR OWN QUESTIONS THAT MAY HAVE COME OUT OF YOUR STUDY |
| EXPERIENCE TOGETHER |

EVALUATION/DISCUSSION QUESTIONS

1. **Given the existence of so many religions laying claim to God, what argument(s) would you use to justify the Christian claim that Jesus is the only way, the truth, and the life?**

---

[39] Jn. 14: 6

4. The Significance Of The Ascension Of Jesus

1. By His ascension, Jesus lives to represent us in heaven

2. The ascension of Jesus is not a metaphor used to describe Jesus' elevation to another level of existence for the Christian believer

3. The ascension makes everything about Jesus a present reality and experience

4. What then, are the benefits of the ascension of Christ to us? The benefits of the ascension of Jesus to us may be seen at five levels. Let us examine them:

   - **Level one**: At the first level, the ascension means that our redeemed human nature has been reunited with the divine nature of God
   - **Level two**: At the second level, the ascension of Jesus means that we have access to heaven
   - **Level three:** At the third level, the ascension implies that Jesus stands before God the Father as our advocate
   - **Level four:** At the fourth level, the ascension means that our prayers have a direct line to God
   - **Level five:** At the fifth level, the ascension of Christ empowers us to live in hope.

5. When we look at the ascension of Jesus from the perspectives of these levels of benefits to us based on the faith we have developed in Him, we are empowered by this added assurance to live out the Christian life and faith on earth

6. The good news today is that because Jesus lives, if you are seeking strength to live day by day, you can find strength in His dominion, power, and authority

7. Because of the life, death, resurrection, ascension and promised return of Jesus, you can have holy confidence in approaching the throne of grace

8. Now tell me, what do you have to lose by believing in the Lord Jesus?

9. You have absolutely nothing to lose by believing in God and accepting Jesus Christ as your Lord and Savior. But you do have salvation and eternal life to gain when you do. What are you going to do about it? Believe on the Lord Jesus and be saved today! Please pray this prayer with me:

    Dear God, I believe that you created me. I believe that You sent Your Son Jesus into the world to die for me. I repent of all my sins. Forgive me of all my sins and by Your Holy Spirit, change me and give me a brand new start. By faith I claim Jesus as my Savior and Lord right now. Come into my heart Lord Jesus; come in today; come in to stay. I pray this prayer in the name of Jesus. Amen!

    I thank God for you my dear reader and friend. Now walk and live in the authority of Christ because you were made for eternity. Hallelujah!

    —

PAUSE FOR REVIEW

SEE QUESTIONS BELOW TO HELP GUIDE YOUR DISCUSSIONS. YOU MAY ADD YOUR OWN QUESTIONS THAT MAY HAVE COME OUT OF YOUR STUDY EXPERIENCE TOGETHER

EVALUATION/DISCUSSION QUESTIONS

1. **"He who descended has also ascended." Take a moment to discuss this statement in light of the reconciling work of Jesus Christ**

2. **Make a list and discuss the benefits of the ascension of Jesus to those who believe**

3. **When we say that someone has nothing to lose by believing in Jesus Christ for salvation, what exactly do we mean?**

CHAPTER TEN

REFLECTIONS, IMPLICATIONS, AND POTENTIAL CONTRIBUTIONS

Devotional Exercise
  Welcome/Greetings
  Sharing of prayer concerns
  Prayer
  Hymn(s) of the day
  Scripture selection(s) for today

(See main text for reflections, implications and potential contributions of this resource)